Judith Okely was born in Malta and studied at La Sorbonne, Paris and a women's college at Oxford. While at Oxford she campaigned for women's membership of the Union and indeed was its first woman member. She has worked as a researcher and lecturer in Social Anthropology at the universities of Durham and Essex and has recently published *The Traveller-Gypsies* and an article on girls boarding schools. This stimulating study of Simone de Beauvoir draws upon Judith Okely's earlier reading of her work in the 1960s and contrasts that response with her re-reading in the 1980s in the light of changes in women's lives and in feminist thinking. Judith Okely currently teaches Social Anthropology at the University of Essex.

VIRAGO PIONEERS are important reassessments of the lives and ideas of women from every walk of life and all periods of history, re-evaluating their contribution in the light of work done over the past twenty years or more – work that has led to important changes of perspective on women's place in history and contemporary life.

Forthcoming Pioneers

Teresa of Avila
Leonie Caldecott

Emily Bronte
Janet Ree

Willa Cather
Hermione Lee

Jane Digby
Rana Kabbani

Eleonora Duse
Eleanor Bron

George Eliot
Jennifer Uglow

Therese of Lisieux
Monica Furlong

Ada Lovelace
Rachel Garden

Margaret MacMillan
Carolyn Steedman

Florence Nightingale
Margaret Walters

Eva Peron
Maxine Molyneux

Sappho
Margaret Williamson

Queen Victoria
Dorothy Thompson

Mary Wollstonecraft
Barbara Taylor

SIMONE DE BEAUVOIR

A Re-Reading

Judith Okely

For Bridget, my mother

Published by Virago Press Limited 1986
41 William IV Street, London WC2N 4DB

British Library Cataloguing in Publication Data

Okley, Judith
    Simone De Beauvoir. – (Virago pioneers)
    1. Beauvoir, Simone de – Criticism and interpretation
    I. Title
    843'.912   PQ2603.E362Z/

    ISBN 0-86068-324-9

Typeset by Rowland Phototypesetting Limited,
Bury St Edmunds, Suffolk
Printed in Great Britain at Anchor Brendon,
Tiptree, Essex

CONTENTS

PREFACE

De Beauvoir gave special inspiration to her women readers in the past, so any assessment of her work cannot be treated as a detached academic exercise. She was much more than a source of facts and theories, she inspired us politically and emotionally. Her books, especially the study of women in *The Second Sex*, evoked a curiously intimate relationship between female reader and writer, between reader and text.

The author's gender and position as a woman were crucial to her women readers who looked for similarities. Her readers were reassured by de Beauvoir's confident tone and were excited by the anger of her polemic. She dared to protest at women's fate. Twenty or thirty years ago she, more than anyone in the west, spoke for many of us women in our scattered silences.

Hers was a female voice. Too often, women readers, faced with a male writer and his heroes, have had to suppress their own difference of gender and imagine themselves as male in relation to the text. But that identification can never be authentic. Similarly, readers of another class, culture and race may tire of reading through the lines of others who are strangers to their own experience. Today, after the creative explosion of feminist writing, a woman reading a woman's text may feel freer to explore the implications of shared gender. Nonetheless, the meeting points depend on the wider context of the individuals and of that re-reading. The reading does not occur in a vacuum but is shaped by history, and the class, age, race and culture of the reader. The text will not read the same for a Black or working-class woman as it reads for one who is white or middle class. Although de Beauvoir's polemic suggested that she spoke universally for all women, much of her description reflects a very specific experience.

The historical period for the reading of the text is also crucial. In the decades since the 1949 publication of *The Second Sex* there have been massive social and economic changes in the west and elsewhere. The women's movement of the 1970s was part of those changes, all of which affect the reading of de Beauvoir's writing. Individual readings will necessarily change. A woman in her late teens reading the text in the early 1960s will have seen it quite differently from the same woman in her forties re-reading it in the 1980s. This very contrast is the background to my appreciation here of de Beauvoir. It is more than an intellectual enterprise; it is also an exploration of the dynamic relationship between reader and author.

Although each reading is solitary, the reader is not unique. My own reading in the early 1960s can be compared with that of the thousands of other women who also read *The Second Sex* with fervour. In order to recall something of de Beauvoir's impact, and to show how the reading has changed, I have introduced evidence from my past reading. There are extracts from my youthful diary and letters. I have added recollections which came through free association during this recent writing. My 1961 volumes of *The Second Sex* have ink underlinings which are a record of my response. More than twenty years later, some of the ideas marked in this way seem banal or simply mistaken, but they speak of the naïvety or conditions of a white middle-class woman of that epoch. I have referred to these traces.

I have felt free to make use of autobiography partly because of a similar concern within some recent feminist and women's writing. Fear of subjectivity is more a masculine attribute which is concealed behind inappropriate claims to scientific objectivity. I am also grateful to a male anthropologist who suggested the idea of a 'personal anthropology',[1] whereby an anthropologist who studies others should first examine the self and its preconceptions.

Mine is not the sole voice used from the past. Embedded in my comments are the voices and recollections of many other women whom I talked with and listened to in preparation for this book. Many preferred to remain anonymous; they were embarrassed by their past innocence. I was fortunate in receiving the testimony of some women from the Third World, not just from the west. The accumulation of their comments sharpened my analysis of how de Beauvoir was once read. In effect, some of the work for this book was akin to anthropological fieldwork.

Given these comments from the past, the account is not smooth and linear. There are staccato interruptions as a reminder of the contrasting readings over time and the changing relationship between text and readers. This recaptured past is compared with the meaning of de Beauvoir's text today, especially in the light of the new feminist writings.

The emotional appeal of *The Second Sex* has changed, if not subsided. For women who read de Beauvoir earlier, this change is also bound up with their individual life cycle and experience through age. Emotions apart, the development of feminist theory means that the intellectual component of the text has to be more rigorously examined. This I have attempted to do in places.

Other judgements, other voices appear in this re-reading of de Beauvoir. My own voice is made impersonal and influenced not just by life experience and changes in feminist practice, but also by the reading of feminist studies and work in anthropology and the social sciences. The 'I' of the past reader has disappeared behind the authority and interpretation of wider reading.

Note

1 See 'The Idea of a Personal Anthropology' David Pocock (1973).

ACKNOWLEDGEMENTS

Many friends and colleagues sustained me in a variety of ways during an uninvited rite of passage and the completion of this study. Some of them are:– Margaret Dickinson, Elaine Okely, Rob Harrison, Bridget Okely, Sue Wright, 'Mother' Jean Campbell, Martin Walker, Belinda Westover, Marie Johnson, Maud Kennedy, Jane Szurek, Cathy Dean, Ros Rundle, Pat Caplan, Alison Scott, Graham Rock, Helen Callaway, Marsaili Cameron, Sonja Ruehl, Jan Hashey, Mika Satow, Signe Howell, Muriel Walker, Joan Knowles, Anita Avramides, David and Marianne Brooks, Angela Trew, Leonore Davidoff, Nat Saunders, Jessie and Nick Bunnin, Maggie French, Connie and Tobie Playel, Kate and Laura Hopkins, Deidre Paulley, and Alan Campbell.

I should like to thank Brenda Corti, Barbara Winstanley and Mary Girling who corrected the manuscript at great speed, Ursula Owen who persisted and encouraged, Marsaili Cameron who made editorial suggestions and Carole Allington who typed the drafts magnificently and always commented.

The photographs on pages 1 and 2 of the illustrated section are reproduced by kind permission of the BBC Hulton Picture Library; that on page 4 by Weidenfeld and Nicolson Archives; page 6 by the Bettmann Archive, New York and page 7 by the John Hillelson Agency.

ABBREVIATIONS USED IN THE TEXT

(references to the French text are my own translation)

MD	Memoirs of a Dutiful Daughter
MJF	Mémoires d'une jeune fille rangée
2nd S	The Second Sex
DS I	Le Deuxième Sexe Volume I
DS II	Le Deuxième Sexe Volume II
PL	The Prime of Life
FA	La Force de l'âge
F Ci	The Force of Circumstance
FC	La Force des choses
ASD	All Said and Done
SCS	She Came to Stay
VED	A Very Easy Death

CHRONOLOGY

1908	*9 January*: Simone de Beauvoir born the first child into a white middle-class Catholic family living in the Boulevard Raspail, Paris.
1910	Birth of Simone's sister, 'Poupette'.
1913	Simone attends a private single-sex school, the Cours Désir. Here she was to meet Zaza (Elizabeth Mabille) with whom she has a profound and loving relationship. She spends every summer holiday at her grandfather's house at Meyrignac in Limousin.
1916–18	Simone realises that she is interested only in being a creative writer. Reading is her great passion.
1922	Simone no longer believes in God.
1925–6	Completes the French school examination (the baccalauréat) in philosophy and mathematics. Leaves school to continue studies at the Institut Sainte-Marie in Neuilly and the Institut Catholique, Paris.
1926	Takes philosophy course at the Sorbonne. She studies literature and philosophy. Friction with her family who consider it a failure to train as a teacher rather than marry. Her bankrupt father cannot provide a dowry for a 'proper' marriage. She had thought of marrying her cousin Jacques.
	She participates in voluntary social work.
1927	Completes her degree or French certificate of letters and philosophy.
1928	Studies at the élite Ecole Normale Supérieure and at the

Sorbonne for her postgraduate 'agrégation' in philosophy. Feels stifled by the amount of study and begins to frequent the bars for adventure. Later resumes her studies with new vigour.

1929   During teaching practice, two of her fellow students are Claude Lévi-Strauss, the anthropologist, and Maurice Merleau-Ponty, the philosopher.

Death of her friend Zaza, after a crisis with her family and Merleau-Ponty whom she hoped to marry.

Meets Jean-Paul Sartre at the Ecole Normale. When he first invites her to dinner, she sends her sister.

De Beauvoir and Sartre achieve outstanding results in the philosophy agrégation examination. They are now qualified to teach. At 21, de Beauvoir is the youngest ever in France to pass this examination in philosophy. It is Sartre's second attempt.

Soon the relationship with Sartre is consummated and consolidated. Sartre suggests their relationship is 'necessary', but they can have other 'contingent' relationships. For de Beauvoir, Sartre corresponds to the dream companion she had longed for since adolescence.

They decide against marriage and parenthood.

Sartre starts National Service.

Simone leaves her parents' home for a rented studio at her grandmother's. Part-time teaching. She starts writing, although not with great confidence.

First trip abroad to Spain with Sartre. The first of many foreign trips with him.

1931   Appointed to teach at a lycée at Marseilles. Sartre appointed to teach at Le Havre. Sartre changes his mind and proposes marriage in order to facilitate appointments in the same place. She refuses and they agree to brief separations.

This first extended period outside Paris, at Marseilles, is something of a liberation on her own. She makes extensive hill walks.

1932   Appointed to a lycée post in Rouen, while Sartre is still at Le Havre.

1933   Beginning of the trio between her former pupil Olga Kosakiewicz, Sartre and herself. This traumatic experience forms the basis for her first published novel (*She Came to Stay*).

Later that year Sartre leaves for 12 months' teaching in

	Berlin. He already has other 'contingent' relationships with women.
	De Beauvoir is reprimanded by the lycée authorities and parents for her sceptical statements on the conventional role of women and for an ironic anti-militarism.
1936	Appointed to the Lycée Molière in Paris.
1937	Sartre appointed to the Lycée Pasteur, Paris. They live on separate floors of hotels and eat out. Both are free of the burden of domestic labour.
	She completes *La Primauté du Spirituel* (*The Primacy of the Spiritual*), a collection of stories which is rejected by two publishers, including Gallimard who were to publish it forty years later (1979) under a modified title.
1938	Begins spending her evenings at the Café de Flore. She and Sartre are oblivious to political events around them.
1939	Teaches at the Lycée Camille Sée, in Paris.
	War is declared. Sartre is drafted into the army.
1940	After the shock of political events which they can no longer ignore, Sartre adopts the notion of commitment, and de Beauvoir 'rallied' to his point of view. After the fall of France and Nazi Occupation of Paris, de Beauvoir, like others, flees Paris and soon returns.
	Sartre is taken prisoner and then released.
	De Beauvoir begins writing alongside others in the Café Flore and the Dôme.
1941	Dismissed from teaching post by Nazis.
	Publication of *L'Invitée* (*She Came to Stay*). She gains recognition.
1944	Liberation of Paris.
1945	With Sartre and a collectivity on the political left, she founds the journal *Les Temps Modernes*. Her play *Les Bouches Inutiles* (*Useless Mouths*) opens. Less successful than as a novelist, she does not write again for the theatre.
	Publication of *Le Sang des Autres* (*The Blood of Others*), acclaimed as the supreme existentialist novel of the Resistance.
1946	Publication of *Tous Les Hommes sont Mortels* (*All Men are Mortal*).
	Sartre says he will spend 3–4 months a year with a woman 'M'. De Beauvoir wonders whom he prefers.
1947	Publication of *Pour une Morale de l'Ambiguité* (*The Ethics of Ambiguity*), a philosophical essay.

She starts working on *The Second Sex*, a massive over-view of women's subordination.

Undertakes lecture tour in the USA.

She commences relationship with the American writer Nelson Algren in Chicago. This was to last four years, sustained by mutual visits and vacations abroad. It would end in bitterness. Algren proposed marriage but de Beauvoir remained 'necessarily' committed to Sartre, and she could not envisage exile from France.

1948   Publication of *L'Amérique au Jour le Jour* (*America Day by Day*).

Advance extracts of *Le Deuxième Sexe* (*The Second Sex*) in *Les Temps Modernes*.

De Beauvoir starts a routine of working at her place (a furnished room) in the mornings and at Sartre's in the afternoons.

1949   Publication of *Le Deuxième Sexe* (*The Second Sex*). A sensation and controversial to both right and left. Thousands of women write to her over the years. 'Above all it lived for them', she says later.

Awareness and debate over the existence of Soviet labour camps. Her enthusiasm for the Soviet Union is questioned. The controversy will be used as a central theme for her novel *Les Mandarins* (*The Mandarins*) which she commences that year.

1950   At a lecture she gives at a club organised by a newspaper seller, in rue Mouffetard, she encounters for the first time a working-class public and records that they are concerned with some of the problems she discusses. There is little follow-up to this direct contact.

Visits Africa.

1951   End of relationship with Algren after visit to the USA.

Acquires her first car.

1952   Benign growth removed from her breast.

Decides to live with Claude Lanzmann, many years younger. This age difference she considered prevented him from challenging her continuing relationship with Sartre, whom she continued to work alongside for part of the day.

Lanzmann alleviates her fear of age and death.

1953   Start of annual summer visits to Rome with Sartre.

1954   Publication of *Les Mandarins* (*The Mandarins*). This novel in which she said she put so much of herself is awarded the celebrated French prize, the Prix Goncourt, although at first it was thought her age (46) would disqualify her.

Start of open Algerian struggle for independence.

Publication of *Privilèges*.

1955   Attends World Peace Congress in Helsinki with Sartre.

Visits China with Sartre.

Moves to a studio apartment in Montparnasse, purchased with money from the Goncourt Prize and which she still inhabited in the 1980s.

1957   Publication of *La Longue Marche* (*The Long March*), an appreciative account of her visit to China.

She reads testimonies of French torture of Algerians.

Invited by students of the left at the Sorbonne to speak on the subject of novels, she is surprised by a warm reception which contrasts with her relatively retiring existence.

1958   Publication of *Mémoires d'une Jeune Fille Rangée* (*The Memoirs of a Dutiful Daughter*) (1st vol. of autobiography).

Speaks at mass meetings to encourage a 'no' vote to the return of de Gaulle to power. The referendum is a resounding 'yes'.

End of relationship with Lanzmann.

1959   She is one of the organisers of a banned meeting protesting at French torture of Algerians. An interview filmed for Canadian television is banned because of her negative views on God and marriage.

Writes preface to a book affirming the right to contraception.

1960   Visits Cuba with Sartre, welcomed by Castro. Visits Brazil and USA.

Campaigns on behalf of Djamila Boupacha, a young Algerian woman tortured by the French.

Publication of *La Force de l'Age* (*The Prime of Life*) (2nd vol. of autobiography). Again a critical and commercial success.

1961   Sartre's flat bombed because of his opposition to French colonialism in Algeria. De Beauvoir and Sartre move to a secret address under a false name, fearing more attacks.

1962   Second bomb attack on Sartre's flat. They move again.

The day of the appearance of the book on Djamila Boupacha with a preface by de Beauvoir, her concierge receives phone calls threatening de Beauvoir's life.

Political agreement to end Algerian war.

She and Sartre visit the Soviet Union, at the invitation of Soviet writers.

1963   Death of her mother.

Visits Czechoslovakia.

Publication of *La Force des Choses* (*The Force of Circumstance*) (3rd vol. of autobiography). Mixed reception – e.g. a review in England berates it for its political stance and 'lack of humour'.

1964   Publication of *Une Mort très Douce* (*A Very Easy Death*), a personal account of her mother's death.

1966   Visits the Soviet Union and Japan with Sartre. All their works have been translated into Japanese and *The Second Sex* was a best seller the previous year.

Publication of *Les Belles Images* (*Beautiful Images*).

1967   Visits the Middle East before the Six Day War. Raises the question of women's rights.

She joins, with Sartre, the Bertrand Russell Tribunal of War Crimes investigating US intervention in Vietnam.

1968   Publication of *La Femme Rompue* (*The Woman Destroyed*).

The May Events – Simone and Sartre support the students and visit the Sorbonne. Again their politics are changed.

1969   Elected to the consultative committee of the National Library under the category 'man of letters'.

1970   Publication of *La Viellesse* (*Old Age*).

De Beauvoir and Sartre sell the left-wing paper *La Cause du Peuple* in the streets to highlight police harassment. They are taken off in a police van and later released.

De Beauvoir joins demonstration of the French Liberation Movement of Women.

Visits Burgundy with young woman friend and philosopher, Sylvie le Bon.

1971   Publication of the Manifesto of 343, which she signed as one of the women signatories admitting to an illegal abortion.

1972   In an interview, de Beauvoir now declares herself a militant feminist. Before 1970 she saw feminism as only reformist and legalistic, now it had become radical. She revised her belief that socialism alone would resolve the subordination of women. Recent socialist examples had shown her that this was not the case.

Joins in demonstrations protesting against crimes against women.

	Publication of *Tout Compte Fait* (*All Said and Done*) (4th vol. of autobiography).
1973	Starts feminist section in *Les Temps Modernes*.
1974	President of the French League of Women's Rights.
	Awarded the Jerusalem prize for writers who have promoted the freedom of the individual.
1978	Film on her life (Dayan and Ribowska).
1979	Publication of her first (previously rejected) set of short stories.
	Death of Sartre.
1981	Publication of *La Cérémonie des Adieux* (*Adieux – A Farewell to Sartre*). Account of Sartre's death and some interviews.
	Death of Algren.
1983	Publication of *Lettres au Castor et à quelques autres* (*Letters to Castor –*[her nickname] *and to some others*). Letters by Sartre to de Beauvoir and some other women, edited by de Beauvoir.
1985	Death of Olga Kosakiewicz-Bost.
1986	Death of de Beauvoir

CHAPTER ONE

EPOCH AND INSPIRATION

She was our mother, our sister and something of ourselves. Her name was a password and slogan. 'That book gave me goose-pimples' said a Japanese woman who read her in the 1960s. She inspired thousands of women as feminists, the majority of whom were white and middle class like herself. Yet in the 1980s a subsequent generation of women, with the luxury of a decade since the rise of the women's liberation movement, react differently. Whereas de Beauvoir's *The Second Sex* (1949) was considered *the* feminist text in the 1950s and early 1960s in the west and beyond, many younger women in a comparable position have never read it. Others confess to having only dipped into the lengthy tome and found it unengaging. They do not recognise themselves there as some women of my generation did. Some of the younger women who have looked at it bristle with anger. I heard a young woman at a conference devoted to de Beauvoir, accuse her of 'having set the movement back many years'. Only a minority of younger feminists, it seems, see her as the inspiration she once was.

It is naïve for a generation schooled in the sixties and after to demand that de Beauvoir should have written as they might write today. It is, however, perfectly correct to scrutinise and reject some of her arguments in the light of subsequent conditions. An assessment of de Beauvoir requires a double reading. Her work can be read in its time, before the revival of feminism with the women's liberation movement, and it can be read differently decades later. Her early readers have themselves changed or been replaced.

A burgeoning industry of scholarly publications tends now to play down de Beauvoir's significance as a writer for feminism. Instead she is being reappraised as a 'doyenne of existentialism' or as a 'stylistically interesting' novelist, regardless of gender, and in this way given renewed respectability as an honorary male among intellectuals. She must really have 'arrived' when an American academic informed us that:

Whatever qualms the male critic might have, Simone de Beauvoir puts his mind at rest: she speaks and writes in such a way that one might forget about the sex of the novelist or the essayist were it not for the constant concern she voices for the cause of women. (Bieber, 1979, p. 17)

At the same time, her autobiography is not read for its own sake, but raided for yet more information about her celebrated male companion Jean Paul Sartre. While academia is busy working over her, feminist theory may have moved on.

This book cannot fully cover all aspects of de Beauvoir's prodigious writing; instead the central focus will be her inspiration to women. Some of us modelled our lives on her pronouncements. There were no other contemporary feminist texts when in 1961, in my late teens, I first read *The Second Sex* and her *Memoirs*. The night before I left home to study in Paris and after the cloisters of an English boarding school, my mother packed J. S. Mill's *The Subjection of Women* in my suitcase. Neither this nor Shaw's *An Intelligent Woman's Guide to Capitalism and Socialism* brought the resonances which de Beauvoir as a woman did. Re-reading her years later, I am astonished at how many phrases and ideas I consciously and unconsciously absorbed from *The Second Sex*. Some of these ideas are no longer appropriate, but they are lying around somewhere in the back of my brain. Her ideas had a similar impact on many other women. The West German writer Alice Schwarzer speaks of de Beauvoir's influence:

In the darkness of the Fifties and Sixties, before the new women's movement dawned, *The Second Sex* was like a secret code that we emerging women used to send messages to each other. And Simone de Beauvoir herself, her life and her work, was – and is – a symbol (1984, p. 13).

This reassessment will draw upon that earlier reading in the early 1960s and will be in part a testimony and a tribute. It is not possible to reconstruct through some formal survey exactly how other young women read her, but I give examples wherever available. From these and from discussions with devotees of my generation I find similarities in the form which our enthusiasm took. The general historical circumstances of the post-war west give some clues, so that the response of isolated individuals can be placed in that context. Elizabeth Wilson has described how in the 1950s and 1960s 'a particular coincidence of economic and political forces in that period created a "culture" . . . in which it was difficult to articulate or to know about any oppression of women' (1980, p. 207). Each individual will have her own story: my observations will possibly fit more closely to the response of white middle-class women in Britain and parts of the United States.

Today de Beauvoir's analysis has been devalued because of the Eurocentric bias concealed in its universal claims. Yet this limitation was paradoxically *The Second Sex*'s strength to women who read it in the Third World, as a woman from the Middle East testifies. De Beauvoir was seen by her to be offering a specific critique of the west:

To many of us who were teenagers (in the 60s), reading European and American literature was *the* way out of a somewhat unhappy existence. . . . We were thoroughly western educated in our own country; on the other hand, we were experiencing a reality as women that almost totally contradicted our adopted western culture and values. The result was a common wish to have been born male. To us, the west was an ideal type, a contrast to what we thought were unacceptable constraints on women in traditional society . . . we continued to believe in the miraculous west until the critical literature began flowing, and Simone de Beauvoir was among the flood.

Only a few of us read her. She was thought to be too intellectual and so she became the challenge to conquer. She challenged the very ideal type that she represented . . . she was able to explain what we felt and experienced as women and at the same time she shattered our myths about the west. Suddenly we began to see the west in the light of women's oppression . . . in the very same terms that we were analysing at home.

. . . She assured us that we were not being 'silly' for thinking or feeling in certain ways. She also opened up the possibilities for alternatives to marriage and children. She became the idol, the ideal type, herself. But she also succeeded in relieving somewhat the contradiction of being anti-imperialist at the same time as being pro-'western' for feminist reasons.

Another testimony is from Mika Gupta who read *The Second Sex* in the sixties in Calcutta where she was born. Her mother was originally Muslim and Urdu-speaking and her father Bengali. 'They had been almost completely absorbed by a colonial mentality' and sent her to an Irish convent where she spoke English:

The writer seemed absolutely foreign in a way that I did not experience English writers. However, de Beauvoir's 'foreignness' also held points of identification in our shared Catholic and middle class upbringing; I remember feeling that her words had a potency because she knew how *I* felt – it wasn't recognition so much as delight in knowing that myself and my girlfriends were not alone in our uneasiness about our relations with 'boys' . . . At the same time I found her alienating . . . her arrogance. There were no spaces into which I could fit my experience as a 'bastard of cultures' . . . I remember being critical on the lines of 'it's all very well for her – she has male support in her "genius"'. My experience was one of isolation. De Beauvoir never offered female solidarity as a tactic. Her use of the term bad faith I found insulting because it didn't take into account where the individual comes from, i.e. the cultural framework. Paradoxically her arrogance was also strengthening because I knew it was 'alright' to question. For these memories I have a gratitude. De Beauvoir made us think of our cultural and class placings, tho' she may not have presented them as problems.

While drawing upon my own and others' past responses, I argue that individual testimony makes sense only as part of a wider canvas. Personal experience is not simply idiosyncratic; its very minutiae can help us to throw light on a specific class of women at a certain epoch. Reading is a subjective relationship between author and reader. That relationship is partly formed by history and by the specificity of the reader; gender, class, race, culture and age are of import. Some categories, like gender, are fixed; others, like culture, are flexible; the experience of each may change over time. De Beauvoir, as a woman scrutinising the conditions of women, elicited an especially heightened response from many of her women readers at a certain epoch. She is as a mother or sister to the female reader, with all the conflicting feelings of adulation or resentment which those relationships entail. There is rarely indifference. To recreate that epoch I draw on the state of naïvety of the young woman reader of those times. Some of that response may seem bizarre today. But the subjective experience of that reader was also a reflection of objective conditions which have since changed.

A reading of de Beauvoir in the 1980s is influenced by the more recent intellectual renaissance of feminism. Today there is a mass of writing on many aspects of women and gender. The arts, humanities and social sciences have embraced and refined studies of women so that it is no longer possible to make pronouncements across all subjects, now that each specialism within women's studies has flowered. In her day, de Beauvoir straddled biology, history, literature, psychoanalysis, political economy, anthropology and philosophy. Few would dare to be so ambitious today.

There are other changes which help to explain a younger generation's detachment from de Beauvoir's themes. Feminism in western society has moved on from certain issues, which are now often taken for granted. Younger women in the majority of western nations, at 'the age of consent', and despite a recent backlash from the political right, may no longer have to argue *in principle* for the right to pre-marital sex, birth control and abortion. In the 1950s and early 60s, by contrast, pre-marital virginity for women was sanctified in the dominant ideology, birth control outside marriage was hard to obtain and virtually *all* abortions were illegal, apart from exceptional cases.

In the immediate post-war decades, middle-class and, in theory, working-class women were expected to embrace the role of full-time married housewife and mother. Earlier, many women had been forced out of traditionally 'male' employment back into 'female' employment when men reappropriated jobs which women had successfully undertaken in Britain and the States during the Second World War. But in practice women continued to be an important part of the external labour force. Post-war reconstruction demanded an increased labour force, including that of women. Inadequate provision was made for a domestic support system, the sexual division of labour was not questioned, so the majority of women were recruited for part-time external

employment (Wilson, 1980). Black women were also to be recruited from the colonies (and within the States) for a limited
range of employment, including, in the case of Britain, jobs
within the expanding welfare state. All the while, public spokes-
men reaffirmed the ideal of the nuclear family with a male
breadwinner and dependent wife. There was a different focus
according to class, as Wilson suggests. The debate about the
employment of working-class women was concerned with the
care of their children, but:

the demand for equality coming from middle-class women seemed to
arouse perhaps even more profound anxieties which ultimately had to do
with it being a challenge to the manhood of men. Working-class women
had after all always been exploited workers, but for a middle-class wife to
work called many conventions into question (1980: p. 53).

'Working mothers' and 'unmarried mothers' were stigmatised
labels. Such people were accused of producing deprived 'latch-
key' children and delinquents. My working widowed mother was
so intimidated by these moral panics that she accepted a charit-
able offer to pay all the expenses of sending my sister and me to a
boarding school. Divorce and 'the broken home', it was said,
destroyed children, but not apparently separation from parents in
élitist schools. While marriage was presented as the ideal,
thousands of women could not attain it even if they wished, partly
because many males of their generation had been killed. These
women were expected to accept both celibacy and lower pay than
their male counterparts. In the post-war family ideal there was no
place for the derided spinster, the single mother, white or Black,
nor even a widow.

   Young women were schooled in the 1940s and 50s in line with
the dominant ideology, however contradictory it may have been
in practice. Middle-class girls, especially, were to respect pre-
marital chastity and to envisage marriage and maternity as their
sole destiny. Paid employment after marriage for both working-
and middle-class women was represented as a break from the
ideal. For the middle-class woman it was seen as a loss of status
and proof of her husband's inadequacy. In addition, the vital
earnings of working-class women were trivialised as frivolous 'pin
money' by public commentators. Dr Spock, Dr Bowlby and

others preached a child-centred world for the post-war mother. Anything like external work should bring guilt. In these circumstances, women were isolated with no group voice to express unease or discontent. Women could not act together to counter the overbearing message of married motherhood. As Wilson suggests, 'it is impossible to overemphasise the importance of marriage as a central and organising idea in both the 1950s and the 1960s' (1980, p. 88).

From somewhere way beyond this domestic claustrophobia, from an exotic bohemia, came a different message: *The Second Sex* argued in confident, defiant tone that woman's fate was invented not inherited. Marriage was depicted as servitude, and housework was exposed in minute detail as unrewarded drudgery comparable to the punishment of Sisyphus. De Beauvoir argued that maternity was not the sugary experience it was made out to be, but painful, constricting and sometimes a disaster. Indeed, the foetus was described as some sort of parasite eating into a woman's independence. In contrast to the stereotype of the derided spinster, de Beauvoir introduced the ideal of an independent woman who would earn her own living, reject marriage and possibly maternity without experiencing stigma and celibacy. Love and sex should be enjoyed in free relationships of equality. The traumas surrounding menstruation and sexual awareness should be openly discussed. Romantic love and emotional dependence on a man were to be pitied, especially when combined with economic dependence. The apparently flattering images of woman as earth mothers and nature goddesses were in effect used to deny her recognition as a human being. Male novelists were criticised for treating woman as object not subject. History, politics and law recorded the subordination of women, not their freedom. The book proclaimed that there was no such thing as 'feminine nature', and a woman's fate was certainly not biologically determined. Nor, in the author's view, could economics and psychology properly explain women's subjection. De Beauvoir's explanation for the causes was not very clear; it had something to do with women always being seen as 'the Other' by men. However, according to the author women were not simply passive victims; they also colluded in their fate, and were guilty of 'bad faith' by turning their backs on a freer existence. Her own

example seemed to show it was possible to choose to be free –
however naïve this may seem now to readers today.

Before the women's movement in the 1970s, de Beauvoir's
detailed polemic appealed to thousands of scattered women
whose domestic and working lives lacked the conditions for
organised solidarity. Her emphasis on individual choice over and
above all external historical constraints drew upon a central tenet
of existentialism and seemed to offer the only possible escape
until, according to de Beauvoir, socialism brought freedom for
everyone, male and female. Meanwhile, a young woman in a
position to seek an alternative would have to detach herself from
those who followed the prevailing conventions. She might even
come to pity them.

The Second Sex was filled with scholarly detail, lacked a
popularising style and therefore reached only a limited readership. More significantly, it reflected the experience of the
cloistered, middle-class and white woman, namely that of the
author, who had had a middle-class, Catholic upbringing. It
struck chords in some readers precisely because they recognised
something of their own condition concealed in de Beauvoir's
deceptively generalised description. This was potentially liberating because what had once seemed like a vague and only personal
discontent was now seen to be linked to a position which others
shared. Yet, whether or not women shared the same class and
cultural privileges, the model of independent woman which the
author herself presented was possible for only a few to imitate.

The identification between author and reader was not of course
inevitable among all western middle-class women. Juliet
Mitchell, who was educated in Hampstead at an élite school
which encouraged girls' academic achievement, at first thought
The Second Sex 'brilliant but somehow applicable only to some
inexplicable predicament of French women' (1984, p. 17). In the
early 1950s in the States, de Beauvoir also seemed culturally
remote to some students. One feminist academic described her
experience to me: 'We dipped into the translation but it washed
over us. France–Europe seemed so far away. In Ohio, de
Beauvoir seemed too erudite.' Also in the States, Carol Ascher,
whose admiration for de Beauvoir has since produced a book, was
too fearful to read *The Second Sex* in 1961. It was greatly prized by

her 'bohemian' room mate who seemed too 'sophisticated' and threatening to Ascher's wish then to conform (1981, p. 108).

In the late 1940s, when the book was written, a counter to the dominant ideology could come only from an exceptional woman who had rejected the ideas of her time. De Beauvoir wrote from the margins of bourgeois life. Only much later in the 1960s were other women to produce feminist critiques from their experience as housewife and mother, and one of these came again from the white middle class: namely Betty Friedan's *The Feminine Mystique* (1963). By contrast, de Beauvoir's position as an exceptional, unmarried and childless woman was the solid base from which she could produce her earlier attack on the dominant culture's notion of the ideal woman. Adrienne Rich notes of childless women from Eliot to de Beauvoir that:

. . . precisely because they were not bound in the cycle of hourly existence with children, because they could reflect, observe, write, such women in the past have given us some of the few available strong insights into the experience of women in general. (1977, p. 252)

De Beauvoir's message from the margins of women's adult life came nevertheless from a powerful cultural centre, that of Paris where she had been given public recognition as philosopher-intellectual, regardless of her sex. The recognition was considerable, especially in view of the respect and power which French society gives to its intelligentsia, in contrast to the traditions of Britain and the States. To her admirers outside France, de Beauvoir's reputation as intellectual gave her an exotic mystique. In what has been criticised (Carter, 1982) as an astonishingly naive statement, Carole Ascher reveals how de Beauvoir's readers found in her a counter to the dominant American view of intellectuals, and in particular, female ones, when she confesses that 'one of the greatest gifts Simone de Beauvoir has given me . . . is her conviction that it is all right to be an intellectual' (1981, p. 225)

Even within France, de Beauvoir was exoticised, thanks to the popular view of existentialism. To young middle-class women abroad she seemed all the more persuasive. Here was an unmarried, childless intellectual who had, it seemed, an unusual arrangement with a 'great philosopher' Sartre. This was an inspiring alternative life to women trapped in the conventional life. Her foreign admirers could indulge in their fantasies of intellectual bohemia in a city which already had a magical allure in Anglo-Saxon mythology. De Beauvoir was herself bemused by the journalistic distortions of existentialism within France and tried to dispel them with little success. But both her critics and her foreign female admirers thrived on a fantasy of this undomesticated other world.

Some publications in the 1950s did indeed express protest at bourgeois conformity not only in France (for example, Camus' *The Outsider*) but also in Britain and the States. A literature of 'loners' and 'outsiders' emerged. As with existentialism, the emphasis was on the individual. These cult figures were male. Women hardly featured as active, changing heroines; they merely serviced the heroes in conventional domestic ways. The cult of the individual rebel was not only a reaction to the overbearing conventions, but also their reinforcement. The loners wanted to keep it that way, not organise with others for change. The 'beat' generation of male heroes in the States travelled countrywide, dabbling in drugs and/or sexual objects in their path (as in Kerouac's *On the Road* and Ginsberg's *Howl*). The 'Angry Young Men' of Britain, as portrayed by Osborne (*Look back in Anger*, Wilson (*The Outsider*) and Braine (*Room at the Top*), often merely sought movement up the class ladder and sometimes used middle-class women to achieve this. A female intellectual risked being the subject of ridicule (see Amis, *Lucky Jim*).

To us foreigners, there seemed in France to be a lighter, less macho atmosphere. This was epitomised by the singer Juliette Greco – a bohemian in brooding black with long uncrimped hair. Greco did not look like a wife, she did not sing like a mother. Her voice was a deeper tone than the high-pitched simper of the acceptable Hollywood heroine. She represented a darker side of sexuality, a freedom from marital bonds, and she sang her melancholia in cafés and makeshift *boîtes de nuit*. De Beauvoir seemed to be associated with that world. Daringly for those days, some of us began to grow our hair long.

The post-war Parisian intelligentsia led a café life which (for the customers) did not include housework, regular meals and washing up. Many lived in cheap hotels. People congregated in commensuality outside the home. The day did not conform to

cf Barbara Ehrenreich

domestic routines. Children seemed to be invisible. Unlike the emerging coffee bars in Britain, cafés were for grown ups, not just adolescents, and alcohol was freely available. Waiters catered for the rootless needs of the intellectuals of either sex. It seemed from the outside that these intellectuals were changing the world through talk and Simone was an equal among the 'great'.

Rachel Brownstein, for example, describes her youth in 1950s America:

Ideally one would be Simone de Beauvoir, smoking with Sartre at the Deux Magots, making an eccentric domestic arrangement that was secondary to important things and in their service. One would be poised, brilliant, equipped with a past, above the fray, beyond it, foreign not domestic. (1984, p. 18)

In 1956 'community' was a laughable pious term evoking Mom and Dad and Apple Pie . . . In our hearts we lived in Paris, my friends and I thinking and inhaling deeply (gitanes) at the Deux Magots confronting Life. (*ibid*, p. 16)

De Beauvoir offered a vicarious identity. She had rejected the housewife's role on principle. Her childlessness without sexual abstinence was a living possibility. With her own livelihood, she had escaped economic and social dependence and her relationship with Sartre seemed, from rumour, to be the ideal. In the 1980s, the feminist Alice Schwarzer continues to maintain that 'this relationship . . . was – and may still be – *the* model of a relationship based on love and freedom' (1984 p. 107). In the past, this is what younger women like myself and others outside the Parisian centre *believed* to be the case, and here I am also dealing with fantasies. Even these cannot be fully recaptured decades later since some have faded and others have assumed a new significance.

Inside my French Gallimard volumes of *Le Deuxième Sexe* (*The Second Sex*) and *Mémoires d'une Jeune Fille Rangée* (*Memoirs of a Dutiful Daughter*) are the words 'Paris Mai 1961'. I read those books in one swoop. This was my second year in Paris, where I had studied for a diploma in French civilisation at the Sorbonne. De Beauvoir gave the final focus to a scholarly apprenticeship and liberation from years at a single-sex English boarding school, from which only one or two were ever encouraged to escape to higher education. In those days, when the percentage of women in higher education was even smaller than today, I was judged 'unworthy' of a British university by the headmistress and pressured not to apply. In Paris, university studies were my emancipation, thanks to my mother who cashed her few savings to send me. Fortunately, student fees, halls and subsidised restaurants were relatively cheap. After a year in Paris, I felt encouraged to apply on my own to a British university. Having gained a place for the following year, my savings from work in an office and factory then enabled me to return to France for a few more months.

The Paris I lived was very different from the fantasy of onlookers abroad. Moreover, foreign women were treated with specific disdain. My first year there I wrote to my sister: 'I find that with the French it is impossible or almost impossible to be taken seriously, they only want to amuse themselves with foreigners – either physically or as a toy.' I had been befriended by Hubert, a student at the élite l'Ecole Normale Supérieure, where de Beauvoir and Sartre had once studied. The aridity and patronising tone of Hubert's colleagues, especially Bruno and Madelin, were disappointing. In March I wrote to my sister Elaine about them:

Because I did not know French literature and French history as they did, I found it impossible to have any discussions with them, I think that that shows the narrowness of their exclusive conversation – they never even discussed abstractly, it was always repetitions of quotations and questions of dates. Hubert admitted that he could not even talk with students of the Sorbonne, because his interests and humour were so refined and exclusive that he got bored with what they said. En tout cas (in any case) he told me that it was crazy of me to expect to be admitted into an intellectual group unless one had had the same education and environment as them.

Thus I stumbled on the very exclusivity that has been used to explain aspects of Sartre's and de Beauvoir's education and subsequent political naivety. Hubert's friends treated me like a formless fool, and thinking I did not understand referred to me as 'la bête'. For a while, I put up with their contemptible behaviour because I wanted to learn as much as I could about the French, especially the intelligentsia. Hubert and I attended a public lecture by Sartre and the first production of Sartre's play *Altona*.

As Hubert's behaviour became more domineering, I stopped seeing him. I acknowledged to my sister my fantasies about intellectualising in Paris:

Voilà the situation of French intellectual circles – like the 18th century salons, all is a closed circle, I had such different ideas of Paris. I imagined sitting in dark night clubs talking and philosophising until the small hours of the morning. O destiny, O life, O eternity, where are we going to, who is leading us, I want to ask. I want to launch myself into the night, I want to feel and touch, I want to take a boat and drift out onto the grey sea.

Yes, I was and I am too naïve.

In that first year out of England, I turned from being a devout Anglican to atheism. There were further changes; I consolidated an earlier lesson from the Suez crisis and the war in Cyprus into socialism and a rejection of colonialism, reaffirmed by the Algerian struggle which was being enacted on the streets around me. Friends had been beaten up and arrested at demonstrations against the OAS.

Eventually I stopped 'going out with men'. In those days the anatomical rules for 'nice girls' separating 'petting' from penetration seemed so ridiculous that I chose abstinence. One man had presumed I was 'experienced' when I had accepted his invitation to stay at his place after my hostel closed. He'd told me there were two beds. So extreme was my ignorance of the mechanics of sexual intercourse that for a while I was convinced that he'd 'taken' my virginity in my sleep! Such naïvety was not unusual for girls of my era. Over breakfast he made me read aloud the seduction scene from Laclos' *Les Liaisons Dangereuses* (*Dangerous Liaisons*). Since an English girl in Paris was regarded as exotic and amoral, there were ample opportunities to lose one's ignorance. Moreover, there was not the public vocabulary to label for ourselves the treatment we received as sex objects.

While my ex-schoolfriends back in England worked towards a 'good marriage', at first I thought myself daring to hover between that and a romantic passion with a great artist. Later it seemed when I read de Beauvoir that she had solved the dilemma of finding a 'great love' while retaining independence. The eighteen-year-old virgin of 1960 who had not yet read de Beauvoir is revealed in the following words to my sister:

Should I marry a solicitor with his feet on the ground, balanced and at ease among people? *or* should I plunge myself into a raw life of passions and devote my body and soul to a Modigliani or Van Gogh who was not understood, who was not accepted, who lived in an imaginary world? – In doing so I would be running away from the world, but I would be living an ideal – a violent self sacrifice for the sake of beauty, art and a tormented soul.

Today that banal, once tortured, dilemma between convention and bohemia is sheer farce! It has become a shameful embarrassment, but it is consistent with that epoch, as Wilson reveals: the 'bohemian myth, capital-A Artist chained to earth mother and beauty/slut' came in the guise of a 'young and sheltered' woman's 'sexual and social liberation' (1980, pp. 152–3). Those were the limits to white middle-class female resistance. The worst is that the 'artistic' escape demanded more self-immolation than marriage; I would be servicing the painter, not doing the painting. The intellectual emancipation of a middle-class eighteen-year-old did not as yet include a glimmer of autonomy. Instead, men had been made the taboo, longed-for objects in a single-sex education. My pubescent fantasy seems now like a living western suttee, but I resurrect it in order to show the kind of soil upon which de Beauvoir's words were to fall. The masochistic self-sacrifice which intoxicated the bourgeois girl of that era was all too well documented in *The Second Sex*. A year later I was to recognise my failings in de Beauvoir's text. In May 1961 I wrote in my diary:

. . . read de Beauvoir's commentary on the woman who occupies herself with literary studies. She who cuts out reality and seeks violent sensations and ecstasies in Literature. The doodler who has to express herself. A surge of terrible clichés comes to my mind. The poor female who writes poetry and paints in order to be different, who regards these additions as extras, as useful additions to catch a man. I have just had another look and have read on. I cried. De Beauvoir's analysis is desperately true . . . The picture of women who 'create' not even consciously to attract a man but subconsciously to please. Their daydream attempts at art are pathetic self affirmations . . .

During my first year in Paris the only remotely feminist book I had read was Mill's *The Subjection of Women*, and I wrote to my mother and sister: 'am pleased to see at long last in print such ideas that have been floating about in my head for months'. A budding feminist would not however, have been warned by Mill of the risks of asymmetry in marriage. We had been led to believe that Mill drew strength from an 'ideal partnership' with his Harriet. (A subsequent feminist critique is that he plagiarised her.) After reading de Beauvoir, I may have been freed from the economic dependency of marriage and the bonds of enforced maternity, yet how many of us were left looking for our Sartre who, as Brownstein also dreamed, 'would look like Albert Camus' (1984, p. 18)? De Beauvoir did not show us how to live independently of the intellectual and psychic support of a 'great man'.

The first threat to her unique partnership with Sartre (in the form of a young rival) was partly fictionalised by de Beauvoir in the novel *She Came to Stay* (1943). In both the novel and real life the partnership somehow survived. Perhaps it was because her young readers had not lived through years of emotional complexities that *She Came to Stay*, in contrast to *The Second Sex* or the *Memoirs*, seemed merely a sophisticated triangle of existentialists' 'free love', rather than a warning of the dangers of emotional dependence on a 'great man'. Certainly this first novel, which I also read in 1961, was understood only as a mathematical puzzle. To a virgin with little experience of relationships with men, the ideal partnership was still a fantasy and untainted by jealousy. The character Anne in *The Mandarins* was perceived as relatively unorthodox rather than trapped in her relationship with her husband, who was older and more powerful. Moreover, in a novel like *The Mandarins*, some of us were more impressed by the political perspective. Here de Beauvoir had given unique insights into dilemmas on the left and thus demonstrated both that she, the female author, could be a member of such circles and that a woman was capable of discussing international issues. Again such minimal 'achievements' might seem banal today.

Meanwhile back in Paris, May 1961, I wrote to my mother and sister on a postcard of Le Pont Neuf – 'Paris en flânant' (strolling through Paris):

How joyful I am to be in Paris you cannot imagine. Now that summer's coming and everybody looks vigorous and gay streaming, herding down Boul Mich. The taste of work has come back in a thrilling outburst. I am reading Simone de Beauvoir . . . equality of women . . . Thanks for details of your job. Mummy you mustn't strain yourself . . . will you have a break between the two jobs? Please assure me that all is running smoothly. I rush back to my books.

Having by then come to terms with my exclusion from the *salons* of L'Ecole Normale and having rejected those in pursuit of a 'loose' foreigner, I took from Paris and French culture what I wished. The Sorbonne offered courses in French literature, history, politics, geography and art. Hours at my desk were broken by walks in the Latin Quarter and throughout Paris – its communities, galleries, markets and streets. In these ways my school lessons were religiously unlearned. In my marginal zone, free of British culture, I was open to the best of another. It was in these circumstances that in May 1961 de Beauvoir's words took me over. Sentence after sentence was underlined. I walked the streets in a daze thinking them through, sometimes weeping. Men would importune me, sometimes even trip me up, when I reacted angrily to their question: 'Vous êtes toute seule mam'selle?' 'Are you all alone miss?' Even this act of walking confirmed de Beauvoir's observations:

the young girl can today go out alone and stroll through the Tuileries; but I have already noted how hostile the street is to her, with eyes and hands lying in wait everywhere; if she wanders carelessly, her mind drifting, if she lights a cigarette in front of a café, if she goes alone to the cinema, a disagreeable incident is soon bound to happen. (*2nd S*, p. 72)

In the margin next to this passage I wrote in 1961: 'What bitter, bitter truth!' Her insights gave me strength.

Then 'Julian', an Englishman, appeared. He was here in his Paris studio to paint. This could have been my passionate Modigliani, for he was disturbingly attractive. But he would not agree with my speeches laden with de Beauvoir concepts. *The Second Sex* had become my armour against anyone who tried to give me the 'eternal feminine' again. De Beauvoir's angry parody had forever exposed this as myth. I recorded in my diary:

. . . How strange that I set out for Paris with the ambition of finding an artist whom I could SAVE, to whom I could dedicate a life laden with self sacrifices. I never found him. This year I meet a painter and joy of joys I am no longer propelled by the morbid desire of self abnegation.

Instead I chose to keep company with close women friends, usually foreigners like myself. My diary records: 'Only women so far have given me the companionship which is valuable and honest. My relationships with men have been shifty' (19 May 1961). My Iranian friend, Mariam, encouraged a scholarly life and political awareness. Margaret, in the same hostel, was soon to go to an English university. De Beauvoir had less impact on her because a socialist egalitarian upbringing had shielded her from the prevailing myths. Her parents, one a professor, the other a qualified doctor, nurtured her with ideas they had formed in pre-war Cambridge. In Paris, we often had to make do with the male literature of French 'loners' like Rimbaud, Camus and Gide. Clutching copies of their books, Margaret and I were later to hitchhike through France as virgin vagabonds.

De Beauvoir also appealed to 'loners'. Her inspiration was more powerful in that it was for women and about women. Her emphasis on individual choice and willpower was gradually imbibed, so that by the time I reached my British university I felt total contempt for the third-year undergraduates who sported diamond engagement rings. I tore out a preface to *The Second Sex* and pinned it on my wall. It seemed that anything could be achieved merely through iron determination. I found some sister feminists but few of my friends and colleagues seemed then to be interested in de Beauvoir. One acquaintance from the Labour club, Anne, recalls that she was no feminist then, because as she described it, she considered 'femininity incompatible with sex equality' (Oakley, 1984, p. 73). She thought of 'a degree as an empty achievement without a husband to go with it . . . My school and my parents had both made it plain that girls should get married. If they could fit in a career as well, that was fine' (*ibid.*, p. 43). My attitude was by then very different. Rejecting any marital overture with a newly acquired distaste, I clung to de Beauvoir's words on my wall:

The women of today are about to dethrone the myth of femininity; they are beginning to affirm their independence in concrete ways . . . Reared by women in the bosom of a feminine world, their normal destiny is marriage, which still in practice subordinates them to man. (*DS* II, p. 8)

Years later my college friend Sheila wrote of me:

A friend of mine called Judith was always talking about Simone de Beauvoir and getting women into the student union. I hated the students' union; political people seemed to be just out to advance themselves. I didn't really understand why she was getting so worked up. My emancipation still seemed to me to be a matter of individual choice, though I was beginning to understand that the emancipation of the working class was not. (Rowbotham, 1973, pp. 17–18)

Ironically, but like de Beauvoir, I also saw women's but not workers' emancipation as mainly a matter of individual choice before a socialist revolution, but I believed in the principle of immediate equality in existing institutions like the Oxford Union, from which all women students were debarred membership. De Beauvoir's polemic inspired me and I helped form a committee to canvass its male members for change. There was extensive opposition, including some from socialist men. An advertisement was placed in *The Times* summoning life members to vote no. The second attempt succeeded and I became the first woman member. The aim was to make a symbolic statement, rather than to move up an élite male hierarchy with its national prestige. Women gained access to the debating hall, dining room, bar and library. Today formal equality in most such institutions is taken for granted by women, and the women's movement can now demand more than equal rights to male privilege.

At that time the controversy over women's right of access to all-male institutions did not encourage students, socialist or otherwise, to think about women's subordination in more general terms. The time was not ripe. My article entitled 'The Spectre of Feminism' was turned down by the male editor of *Isis* in 1962 as 'insufficiently anecdotal'. While he was looking for sensational revelations about women undergraduates, it should really have been criticised for its clumsy paraphrasing of de Beauvoir (Okely, 1963).

There were other more specific areas where de Beauvoir's discussions became increasingly relevant. Paradoxically, far greater controls on women's sexuality were exercised in my British university than in Catholic France. All women at our college had to sign an undertaking not to marry during their three years' study. This certainly did not mean that pre-marital sexual relationships were regarded as the alternative. A woman student was sent down from university for being found in bed with her boyfriend *during* the male visiting hours (2–6 p.m.). She lost her grant and could not obtain a reference to any other university. The man, by contrast, was sent away from his all-male college for two weeks. Presumably, only virgin women were permitted the fruits of knowledge. Academic studies were seen as the route to a spinster celibate career for a tiny female élite, or as a cultural 'dowry' for a delayed marriage (see also Wilson, 1980, p. 33). The student's expulsion received national publicity and the college and principal were besieged by the press. Women students of those times in an all-female institution showed no enlightened solidarity. One (who subsequently progressed to a permanent university fellowship) initiated a petition supporting the college's action, while others of us signed a counter petition. At Cambridge, my friend Margaret also circulated a protest petition which some women refused to sign because they said the student should have realised that a college named after a nun and saint would demand chastity.

A lecturer in English, David Holbrook, wrote an article in our university magazine *Isis* in 1962 defending the college's decision to send down our colleague for pre-marital sex and declared that the experience of sexuality should be restricted to the purposes of reproduction. With astonishing naïvety, he insisted that a celebrated Indian temple sculpture which showed men and women in a variety of coital embraces expressed spirituality as opposed to anything carnal. The gamekeeper Mellors in *Lady Chatterley* was condemned for his 'vulgarity'. When some of us jointly signed a critical reply written by Devra, a college friend, the university responded by banning all discussion of sexuality in student magazines. My friends and I were soon stereotyped as public sex objects by university males and the media. Another student in a college secretly married after she became pregnant. When this was discovered, she was banished to a town twenty-five miles from the university and forbidden access to lectures, libraries, and tutorials during the term before her finals. A scholar with great potential, she wept throughout her exams for which she was allowed to make the return visit. The next year, a third member of the college concealed her pregnancy under a vast coat lest she be expelled. While continuing to eat in hall and live in college, she avoided all contact with the doctor and pre-natal clinics. A few days after finals, she complained to the college nurse of 'terrible pains' and gave birth. Whereas the woman had risked her health, baby and degree, the father was the subject of amused admiration at his viva examination.

Although pre-marital sex, maternity and marriage were forbidden by the college, being 'engaged' was approved and possibly regarded as the ideal state, since the authorities were still ambivalent about the aims of higher education for women. When I asked for a weekend's leave of absence to attend an anthropology conference in London with my mother as 'chaperone', permission was refused, but I was informed that if, for example, I wanted to say goodbye to a hypothetical fiancé 'flying to Australia from London airport' I would have been allowed a day's – but presumably not a night's – absence. Thus the safeguarding of a woman's marriage was considered by élite women academics as more important than any intellectual ambitions. All this was entirely consistent with de Beauvoir's comments on the stigma of the 'blue stocking' and the caution which condemns women to intellectual mediocrity (*DS* II, p. 14).

The all-female college authorities seemed even more hopelessly naïve than we were about the practicalities of sexual intercourse. In earlier years, any woman receiving a male visitor had to push her bed out into the corridor. A similar concern was to be found in the States; at Smith College in the 1950s, according to one student, the rule was that when a woman student received a male visitor in her room 'all four feet' had to remain touching the floor. Rigid gender segregation with a view to controlling sexual relations was also enforced in French universities; for example, many women's halls of residence (including the one I had once lived in) forbade male visitors to women's rooms at all times. It is not surprising then that in Paris 1968 the Nanterre students, who precipitated the mass protests which challenged de Gaulle's government, included in their actions a sex education campaign and the mass entry of women's hostels by male students. This resulted in a repeal of many restrictions.

This catalogue of constraints on the sexuality and experience of women in higher education before the women's liberation movement reveals a very different picture from what might have been presumed to be in the centre of enlightened privileged circles. The restrictions were often no less severe on middle-class women outside higher education. The ideal of pre-marital sexuality among working-class women may have been less rigid, but birth control and abortion both before and after marriage were even more difficult to obtain (see Wilson, 1980, pp. 90–100). Thus de Beauvoir's demand for women's sexual autonomy and control over reproduction had dramatic impact in those early years and again in the 1960s. Her suggestions were in no way linked to any programme of mass promiscuity nor to any deceptive freedom for women to be treated as sexual objects. Indeed, her very discussion of the European myth of woman as 'Other', mysterious and erotic object already gave warnings of the kind of problems which feminists were to highlight after the late-1960s 'sexual revolution'. Then, freed of some of the ideals of pre-marital chastity and with greater access to birth control, women found that they were treated with 'sexist' contempt by men in the civil rights movement. Their experience led them back to feminism (see Mitchell, 1971) and to de Beauvoir.

Today, those radical feminists who declare that women sleeping with men are, under all circumstances, collaborating with the 'enemy' will doubtless see an older generation's demands for women's independent control over their heterosexuality as a mere diversion. They might, however, be sympathetic to our objections to the policing of women's fertility. Although de Beauvoir idealised the heterosexual couple, at that time her sympathetic (but occasionally stereotyped) discussion of lesbianism was against the grain and elicited predictable controversy. As in her general discussion of woman, de Beauvoir denied that lesbianism could be explained by any biological, psychological or social determinism. Contrary to the ¡clichés and pathological explanations of her day, she rejected any suggestion that it was a 'perversion' but saw it as a freely adopted attitude. As with all human behaviour, it could involve either self-deception or freedom (*DS* II, ch. 4).

CHAPTER TWO

THE MAKING OF A PIONEER

The first volume of de Beauvoir's autobiography *Memoirs of a Dutiful Daughter* (1958), written after *The Second Sex* and her more celebrated novels, stands as a gift to feminist consciousness. This is the testimony and account of a woman who broke from a claustrophobic bourgeois upbringing, defied most of its lessons and achieved a measure of freedom, despite the constraints demanded of her gender and class.

The *Memoirs*, although non-fiction, can be placed alongside a tradition in literature which includes novels of apprenticeship. The passage from childhood and youth to adulthood is a crucial theme in much of this work. Key choices are made and struggles won or lost at such crossroads. This theme occurs in the writing of a number of celebrated novelists, often male, many of whom have drawn on their own autobiography; for example, Lawrence in *Sons and Lovers*. Balzac plots the dangers which young men encounter when they move from the provinces to Paris; for example, in *Le Père Goriot* (*Father Goriot*) and *Les Illusions Perdues* (*Lost Illusions*). De Beauvoir herself states that Balzac projected the story of his own youth into his heroes (*DS*, I, p. 291). Joyce, in *Portrait of the Artist as a Young Man*, recreates his Catholic upbringing and self-imposed exile. Tolstoy's *Childhood, Boyhood and Youth* is partly his own story.

While there are numerous examples of male writers describing the spiritual progress and self-fulfilment of the young man, very few of them have been concerned with those aspects of a woman's experience. For women, the texts by women about women have been powerful. George Eliot's Maggie Tulliver in *Mill on the Floss*, Alcott's Jo in *Little Women* and Brontë's heroine in *Jane Eyre* were also important in de Beauvoir's own apprenticeship. Yet none of these heroines represents a triumph of female autonomy – Maggie drowned, Jane married her master, although his power was tempered by blinded dependence, and Jo married the paternal professor.

De Beauvoir's early writing was concerned with the crucial struggles of the girl or young woman. As a collection of stories based partly on her own experience and that of her contemporaries, it was also a testimony to her schoolfriend Zaza. The latter's untimely death had been induced by conflict between her family's demands for an arranged marriage and her love for a young man. Unfortunately, this work by de Beauvoir was rejected as 'unoriginal' by publishers in the late 1930s. It finally appeared in the late 1970s as *When Things of the Spirit Come First* (1979, 1982) and is an important contribution to the literature of adolescent struggles lost or won. The publisher's male reader who had rejected the stories judged them in terms of their ability to portray a broad tableau of social mores, something which he considered other writers had already done. He did not appear interested in the gender specificity and nuances of her psychological studies, which de Beauvoir defended as unique (*FA*, p. 336). Her intention had been to limit herself to things and people whom she knew: 'I would try to present a truth which I had experienced personally' (*FA*, p. 229).

De Beauvoir wanted to demonstrate 'through individual narratives, something which went beyond them: the profusion of crimes, whether great or small, which spiritual mystifications conceal' (*FA*, p. 230). The masochistic outlets which women seek from religious and sexual oppression were explored. There are wise virgins and foolish ones; some who succumb, others who try to break free, some who learn too late and one or two who can benefit from their new knowledge. One of de Beauvoir's young heroines, Marguerite, based on the young Simone, finally frees herself from 'mysteries, mirages and myths' (*FA*, p. 232). A brilliant portrait of a provincial school teacher's influence over adolescent girls and her escape into aesthetic fantasy predates a similar politically right-wing character, Spark's celebrated Jean Brodie (1961).

De Beauvoir's use of autobiography in her portrayal of adolescent struggles is not a simple transcription of persons and events from her life. Some of the characters are selves she escaped, others are selves she succeeded in becoming. For example, Marcelle, who fails to free herself and marries Dennis (based on her cousin Jacques whom she nearly married in real life), is represented as the sister of the then liberated Marguerite. Nevertheless, the word 'I' is used only for the latter. Some incidents here transposed in fiction later become the basis for generalisations in *The Second Sex* or are found realistically documented in the *Memoirs*. In all three forms of presentation, some women readers may find aspects of themselves, but their opportunity to relate to adolescent girls' struggles in de Beauvoir's fiction was delayed for forty years by the literary canon. (See also Francis and Gontier 1979, pp. 275–316).

Meanwhile, through the 1960s and 1970s and up to the present, the entirely autobiographical *Memoirs* have been a key text for the female reader contemplating her own upbringing and struggle for freedom. De Beauvoir, as female writer and thinker, presents a model of fulfilment compatible at least with the gender of the female reader, and it sometimes echoed their experience. She gives the specific details of women's oppression and we trust her because she shows that she has lived it and emerged with relative freedom. In the post-war period here was a living example, whereas the inspiration available from Eliot and Brontë belonged to the nineteenth century. The autobiographical recognition between the female writer and reader is greater when each belongs to the same era. Ellen Moers writes of the impact of Charlotte Brontë in the nineteenth century, when Victorian women listened to

the new and dramatic female voice of *Jane Eyre, an Autobiography* . . . the unknown author had put certain basic female experiences and emotions for the first time . . . said Harriet Martineau . . . 'I was convinced that it was by some friend of my own, who had portions of my childish experience in his or her mind'. (1978, p. 65)

However inspiring the masculine models of freedom given by

male writers, ultimately they cannot work for the woman reader. The past, present and future for a young man have little in common with those of a young woman. An equivalent modern writer in the English language, Doris Lessing, portrayed a heroine working through struggles of a later period in adulthood in *The Golden Notebook* (1962). Although she declared it 'was not a trumpet for Women's Liberation' (1971), it was seized upon in the 1960s as a role model and testimony of an adult woman's progress.

At the Sorbonne in 1960 I read the nineteenth-century novels and the modern writers on the syllabus, like Proust, Gide and Rimbaud who offered accounts of the young man's passage to adulthood and sometimes models of freedom. But any potential identification between female reader and male hero was ultimately inauthentic. By contrast, de Beauvoir's *Memoirs* offered a personal blueprint precisely because she was female and not a character from fiction.

As with a re-reading of *The Second Sex*, there are different passages in the *Memoirs* which I would now underline, yet those lines underscored in my 1961 copy are less likely to be discredited today. An individual's explicit autobiography and personal experience cannot be written off, cannot be denied in the same way that a theory about women in general may be faulted with the passage of time. When the writer makes the 'I' explicit, the reader recognises its specificity, and decades later cannot discredit the self described merely because it belonged to a different epoch, although the interpretation may alter. If the autobiography is sufficiently probing it demands that the reader probe her own past. De Beauvoir first invites the reader to question the making of their mutual female identity. Secondly, she provokes the reader into making comparisons and contrasts across time and space, looking at gender at a specific period and from the standpoint of a certain class, race and culture. Thus after the advent of the women's movement, the *Memoirs* continue to evoke considerable response from a younger generation.

A young English anthropologist, Marie Johnson, embarking on fieldwork in a foreign country in the late 1970s, took with her de Beauvoir's autobiographical volumes and describes their effect, especially that of the *Memoirs*:

It was the most intense time of my life so far. I had great freedom and felt massive obligations, was thrown on my own resources and revelled in the responsibility of making all my own decisions but was at times tentative and uncertain. As far as it is possible to say it was then that I fully acknowledged that one day I must die. When I was engaged in my own autobiographical reconstruction, I read Simone de Beauvoir's and it is not surprising that the first volume meant most to me. It dealt with the periods, childhood and adolescence, with which I was coming to terms. Today five years later I cannot recall individual incidents in the book. I just remember a general feeling that however disparate our lives Simone de Beauvoir described what I felt while growing up. Is it pretentious to say that the *Memoirs*, more than any other book, played a part when I recreated my past in a place when I finally left childhood?

At a time of youthful uncertainty, whatever the changes of decades, de Beauvoir's triumph is one with which the female reader may wish to empathise.

My 1961 ink marks reveal several themes. There are instances where I was able to recognise similar experiences, some of the most incidental kind, like her description of the Paris metro or her references to places I had also visited in France. I was grasping at any and every similarity in experience rather than acknowledging differences. Assuredly we came from different cultures; my time in Paris and France was of months not her years.

The major similarities concerned a white, middle-class, gender-segregated education and the weight of an ideology which demanded marriage as the only female vocation. De Beauvoir's way out of these constraints was to seek lofty detachment. She had to see herself as exceptional in order to dislocate herself from a conventional feminine future. In those days this seemed to be the only avenue for women with any intellectual enthusiasms. Throughout, there are references to her self-imposed isolation. On page one the words 'à l'abri' (sheltered) (which I underlined) describe how she learned about the world from a sheltered viewpoint, but gradually she gains autonomy, which is also painful. As she grows, she learned that she was 'condemned to exile'. This I also underlined.

Today it is possible to see the embedded influences on de

Beauvoir of her reading in psychoanalysis and existentialism – the infant's necessary experience of separate identity of self and existentialism's emphasis on each individual's aloneness, regardless of context. Then I responded with gut recognition. The aloneness and uniqueness which de Beauvoir describes in herself become sharper later in girlhood and are not simply a bland application of existentialist theory, which also confronts those themes. Her transition from a sheltered enclave in the family to exile is not merely an inevitable growing up, but also her exile from the gender values and life which her family offered. Like Joyce's hero she chooses exile. Unlike him, her exile is everything but geographical; Paris remains her permanent base. Whereas as a woman she had to exile herself from a specific gender identity, neither Joyce nor his hero had to exile himself from conventional masculinity.

According to a study of gender differences in autobiographies, Jelinek (1980) finds that men are more likely to mythologise their childhood and depict it as an idyll of innocence. Women's description of their childhood has little such nostalgia: its traumas are remembered, although treated with detachment and irony. There may be self-doubt. De Beauvoir exposes her childhood as problematic rather than idyllic, yet she emerges in triumph. Her discussion of sexuality is more open in the volume devoted to her childhood and adolescence than in her later autobiographies. Since her sexuality is then mainly self-centred, she does not risk betraying the confidences of others. Once her sexuality brings intimate relationships, her autobiography respects others' privacy, especially Sartre's.

The untainted confidence of her autobiography, while in accord with dominant male conventions in autobiography (see Jelinek, 1980), aroused anger in some quarters. Referring to the *Memoirs*, Mary Ellmann suggests that 'the fear of similarity rather than of emulation may account for the particularly fierce dislike which men express for primarily decisive women writers like de Beauvoir' (1979, pp. 207–8). The same woman critic does not fully support that decisiveness but sees it as borrowing a certitude belonging to the nineteenth century: 'the defect of Simone de Beauvoir is the authority of her prose: the absence of hesitation in hesitant times amounts to a presence, a tangible deficiency' (*ibid.*,

p. 166). Yet it was this very certitude which appealed to many of her women readers in the past when there were few other authoritative female voices.

This confidence therefore either provoked or inspired. It seemed in 1961 that the *Memoirs* offered a recipe for escape despite the fact that de Beauvoir's kind of 'success' was largely unobtainable for most women. The narrative was of a triumphant destiny attained not by good fortune but by individual willpower, the intellect and reasoned choice. The emphasis on an individual's power to choose, whatever the specific historical conditions, was the basis of Sartre's argument with Marxism, and in the 1970s de Beauvoir modified it, specifically in relation to women and those of a different culture and race. (She recognised that, at least in the extreme case of women in a harem in an Islamic culture, talk of women having the power to choose freedom from subordination was inappropriate.)

In her own case, she does not analyse the cluster of circumstances which facilitated her special independence. In the 1980s I can see these embedded in her text. In 1961, I responded to the stronger message that willpower should eventually become paramount. My opinion was later modified partly because the class privileges of the tiny minority of women who had won a place at my British university presented a competing explanation. They had the luxury of choice, but even these university women followed rather than chose their fate – many who, by their final year were engaged to be married. Degrees became mere cultural dowries. The first rumblings of discontent in the early seventies among my contemporaries who had chosen marriage and domestic dependency appeared at first surprising. Why had they not read the available warnings in de Beauvoir long ago?

The privileged position from which de Beauvoir could make her choices included her ethnic and class origins and her position in the family. Simone, a white European of a colonising nation, had the added advantage of being born and brought up in Paris, the centre of French culture. Here were the élite universities, more especially the Ecole Normale Supérieure, to which those from the provinces also aspired, but where the young Simone did not have to overcome the same shock of unfamiliarity as might a student selected from the provinces. The cultural divide between the French metropolis and provinces was greater than in any other western nation.

The young Simone's social class guaranteed a specific and private education, so facilitating university entry despite the constraints of gender. She had the domestic conditions for reading; there were books in the home. True to the bourgeois French tradition, her father was widely read in the arts and cultivated similar interests in his daughter. Paradoxically, the downward mobility of her family became an opportunity because it meant that her father could not provide the necessary dowry for his daughters and Simone was compelled to train for her livelihood. The father's failure in his own terms lost him all power to consolidate for her a conventional bourgeois future.

Naturally, there were innate abilities for the young girl to develop; these should be taken as given in the case of the young woman who passed the philosophy postgraduate or agrégation examination. Accidents of birth also affected de Beauvoir's future. Simone was born the elder daughter and followed not by a brother but by one sister. Given her position in the family, she was treated as an honorary son and she received some of the privileged attention normally reserved for males.

The *Memoirs* are a rich source for the study of gender construction and the making of a woman 'pioneer' who is both identified as a woman and yet separated from the majority of women, working class, middle class, and women of another race and culture. I have selected three major aspects of de Beauvoir's childhood: her relationships with her father and mother and the girl's experience of space and nature. These aspects both throw light on her adult life and provide significant insights into the formation of other women. Individual experience is not free of the generalised historical conditions which affect gender.

● Honorary son but not heir

It seems no coincidence that other women who have achieved exceptional status in largely male spheres also had no brothers. Golda Meir, Indira Gandhi and Margaret Thatcher, the first woman prime ministers of their respective countries, were without brothers, and the latter two were tutored for political power by their fathers. They were honorary sons and of course not necessarily feminists. The ensuing discussion should not be misread as a 'solution' to the subordination of women (see Heilbrun, 1979, ch. 4). Individual achievement by 'exceptional' women may merely affirm the dominant system. Moreover, as de Beauvoir's case reveals, women brought up as honorary sons experience profound contradictions. De Beauvoir's path to the intelligentsia was marked by contradictions since her father set limits to her education under his tutelage and hoped ultimately that she would cement a 'good marriage', and her ambivalence towards her mother and women in general was extreme. If the sibling who came after de Beauvoir had been male, interest in her education and intellectual development would have been weakened, but as brotherless daughter, she was treated more like a son and escaped a rigid gender demarcation. De Beauvoir acknowledges that with

no brother; there were no comparisons to make which would have revealed to me that certain liberties were not permitted me on the grounds of my sex; I attributed the restraints that were put upon me to my age. Being a child filled me with passionate resentments; my feminine gender never. (*MD*, p. 55)

Her cousin Jacques provided a gender contrast as she grew up, but he was not a brother in the centre of the family, instead someone to see as a future husband.

De Beauvoir's family had been hoping for a son, so her younger sister, Poupette, had been a 'disappointment'. Her sister was doomed merely to follow after Simone who, as elder, had done everything before and seemingly better. De Beauvoir says that she was glad of the presence of her sister, but Poupette was not a major rival. Being the eldest, she found that her father took more interest in her progress than in that of her sister, who sensed this and learned by heart the names of all Napoleon's marshals to impress her parents – to no avail. In the opening paragraph of the *Memoirs*, she declares that although she was at first jealous of her sister, this did not last long: 'As far back as I can remember, I was always proud of being elder; of being first' (*MD*, p. 5). She might have felt this differently if a 'first son' had succeeded her.

In de Beauvoir's infancy we find the familiar phenomenon of

the absent father; that is, he is invisible during most of the baby's waking life. Soon there are traces of the daughter trying to attract men, if not specifically her father. As the *Memoirs* progress, we find the standard incestuous struggle by the daughter who tries to seduce the father.

De Beauvoir's father made significant interventions once she went to school and he became interested in her progress.

He seemed to me to belong to a rarer species than most men . . . No one . . . was nearly as funny, as interesting and as brilliant as he; no one else had read so many books, or knew so much poetry by heart, or could argue with such passion. (*ibid.*, p. 25)

Already he was seen by her as someone to admire and imitate. Monsieur de Beauvoir did not quite fit any conventional mould. He chose to excel in intellectual pursuits and would have preferred to be an actor. Suspended between the aristocracy and bourgeoisie, he became a lawyer and sought consolation in amateur acting.

It might be argued that the father's close attentions to his daughter's education at home and at school were nothing special. After all, Monsieur de Beauvoir encouraged his wife to read. Madame de Beauvoir had had a sheltered youth, was eight years younger than her husband and accepted second place. So was Simone's experience merely the same limiting refinement for ladies? The kind of encouragement bestowed on his wife could well have been all that the father intended for his daughters, but the eldest received unusual attention during some crucial formative years. Unlike the wife/mother, the daughter could act upon her knowledge and change in adulthood.

The father saw Simone as having a male intellect: 'Papa used to say with pride: "Simone has a man's brain; she thinks like a man: she *is* a man"' (*MD*, p. 121). In everyday life, Simone found that everyone treated her like a girl.

De Beauvoir traces how her father directed her education. He corrected her writing and formed her taste in literature. They read aloud to each other. He was pleased to answer her questions and did not intimidate her. The young Simone felt that he treated her as an adult, that he raised her 'up to his level', whereas her mother treated her as a child. In some contexts, she was grateful for her mother's approach because her mother accepted her for what she was: just a child. But on the other hand, Simone was flattered most by her father's praise.

In these descriptions and memories we gain the impression that Simone felt that she was not so much the girl destined to be different from other girls but rather was Papa's potential successor: an equal, regardless of her gender. Simone was allowed to penetrate his private abode, his study. She worked at his desk, was rebuked if she left it untidy 'like a child'. She recalls the little niche under Papa's desk where she once used to hide herself away (*MD*, p. 81). The same niche is introduced, on page one, as her shelter in infancy. Solitude exalted her, she says, but de Beauvoir does not observe that nestling under Papa's desk is more than mere isolation. The space contains a fantasy of intimacy with Papa. That incestuous intimacy with him at his work place, the womb of his study, was linked to the image of the father as intellectual with whom she sought to identify.

'Without striving to imitate' her mother, young Simone was 'conditioned by her' (*MD*, p. 41). This involuntary influence contrasts with the more explicit imitation of her father. From early on she rejected the idea of having babies and was averse to marriage (*ibid.*, p. 87). When she played at nurses it was to 'bring in the wounded from the battlefield in heroic fashion' (p. 56) but not to look after them. She would accept a maternal role in games so long as it excluded nursing aspects. Both then and in adolescence she was aware of the burdens of domestic labour. While putting away the dishes, she consoled herself that her life would lead somewhere; she was not destined for the housewife's fate. This did not, however, entail a wholesale rejection of her female identity. In her games, plans and daydreams she never changed into a man, but imagined herself fulfilling her destiny as a woman. She simply adapted this female identity to her liking.

From her mother, Simone learned piety and self-restraint. By contrast, her father was an unbeliever: 'My intellectual life – embodied by my father – and my spiritual life – expressed by my mother – were two radically heterogeneous fields of experience' (*MD*, p. 41), and:

my father's individualism and pagan ethical standards were in complete contrast to the rigidly moral conventionalism of my mother's teaching.

This imbalance, which made my life a kind of endless disputation, is the main reason why I became an intellectual. (*ibid.*, p. 41)

In this passage, de Beauvoir appears to suggest that it was merely the act of disputation itself which made her an intellectual. She omits to observe that becoming an intellectual is opting for her father's side. Only a few lines earlier she describes how he embodied her intellectual life. The 'endless disputation' was really a struggle between siding with her father as male and her mother as female. She did not want to be identified as a male, but she liked some of the qualities attributed to the male alone. No wonder that she grabbed at models for imitation, albeit fictional, who seemed to have resolved the problem; for example, Jo in *Little Women*: 'I identified myself passionately with Jo, the intellectual' (*ibid.*, p. 90), a tomboy who hated sewing and housework and loved books.

Although de Beauvoir's *Memoirs* were written in her forties, the detail is extensive enough to suggest some of the contradictions which the young Simone faced, and which the adult autobiographer does not recognise. Insofar as the father perceived his daughters as sexually feminine, Simone was not treated as the honorary son, yet in her pre-pubescent, androgynous state, she needed only to please and captivate him as 'innocent' little girl by her intellectual progress.

The pre-pubescent daughter experienced intense emotions towards her father. When he took her out to the theatre, what pleased her most was being alone with him; it was 'intoxicating'. (Again this intimacy is forged in an intellectual context.) In her pre-pubescent days, Simone did not want to grow up and leave home. When she had loved her parents for twenty years, how could she leave them for an unknown man? It was not that she saw marriage as servitude, it was the '*promiscuity* of marriage' that repelled her (*ibid.*, p. 73, my emphasis). This is a strange choice of word. It is as if her bed were already peopled with a phantom occupant – the father. The subsequent description of her adoration for Christ whom she gazed at with 'eyes of a lover' has resonances with her feelings for her father (*ibid.*, p. 73).

The relationship between her father and Simone could not be continuous. The androgynous cygnet was not to become the son who could continue an unbroken identification. He taught her to admire him. She had responded to his enthusiasms by striving to imitate him while at the same time wanting to be his beloved. But for all his unorthodox touch of bohemianism, Monsieur de Beauvoir was 'a true representative of his period and class', a nationalist who loathed foreigners, was anti-semitic and based 'private morality' in the family (*ibid.*, p. 35). Married women were to be faithful and young girls virgins. With such rigid views on marriage and sexuality for women, he did not envisage anything different for his daughters. As her sexuality became explicit with puberty, the relationship between father and daughter changed dramatically. After her first period, he joked publicly about this secret which she had thought was reserved between women. Before, she had always thought of herself as a 'purely spiritual being' in relating to him. Now she was ashamed that he could consider her as a 'mere organism' (*ibid.*, p. 101). She had thought of herself with him as neither body nor soul but just 'mind' in a 'limpid atmosphere where unpleasantness could not exist' (*ibid.*, pp. ·36–7).

The adult writer carries over her painful feelings during that time. She recalls how 'with complete absence of tact' her father would 'pass remarks about my complexion, my acne, my clumsiness, which only made my misery worse' (*ibid.*, p. 101). Her confidence was shattered dramatically when she did not appear to live up to her father's expectations:

As long as he approved of me, I could be sure of myself. For years he had done nothing but heap praises on my head. But when I entered the 'difficult' age, he was disappointed in me; he appreciated elegance and beauty in women. Not only did he fail to conceal his disillusionment from me, but he began showing more interest than before in my sister, who was still a pretty girl. (*MD*, p. 107)

In a revue, Poupette, to her father's delight, played 'Queen of the Night', a part loaded with erotic symbolism. De Beauvoir's account seems to suggest that her father rejected her because she did not apparently turn into some beautiful swan, whereas her sister retained her prettiness before puberty.

There is no objective evidence that de Beauvoir was ugly, yet the adult writer appears to be convinced that this was the explanation for her father's behaviour. Instead it seems that as her sexuality became explicit, any feelings towards her as sexual object had to be most vigorously renounced. His apparent protestations as to her ugliness could be self-deceptive when he turned to his youngest daughter, with whom his relationship would remain 'innocent'. The advent of Simone's puberty was dangerous not because she apparently lost her feminine looks but because she became overtly feminine. The father was confronted with her as feminine offspring, not as honorary son. Instead, Simone felt and believed herself to be found wanting and was jealous of her sister. Mortified, Simone asked her sister if she was really ugly; would she ever grow up to be a woman 'pretty enough to be loved'? Poupette did not understand because she was 'accustomed to hearing my father declare that I was a man' (*ibid.*, p. 146). While her sister was newly favoured, de Beauvoir, as adult autobiographer, recognises that her real rival was her mother. She hoped for a 'more intimate relationship' with her father at this time, but he would not collaborate (*ibid.*, p. 107). These rivalries were to be re-enacted in adulthood.

So, at adolescence, Simone found herself isolated from her father. There was no progressive identification between father and elder daughter, once honorary son. The offspring was now marriageable, but the father could not fulfil even these ambitions for his daughter since he was near bankrupt, with no dowry to marry off his daughters into high society. It was for that, de Beauvoir thought, he intended her polished education.

De Beauvoir discovered that she failed in her father's eyes in more than one way. However much she had benefited intellectually from her father's ambitions, she could not fulfil them according to any male ideal. She often heard her parents complain: 'What a pity Simone wasn't a boy; she could have gone to the Polytechnique'! (*ibid.*, p. 177). Her father advised the civil service, where at least she would have a pension. Instead she chose to be a teacher, a profession he despised, partly because he feared the radicalism of full-time intellectuals. Ironically she had followed his interests too seriously. It seemed that the only way she could satisfy her father's wounded pride was by being exceptional and by accumulating diplomas in superhuman quantity:

His insistence on this point convinced me that he was proud to have a brainy woman for a daughter; but the contrary was true; only the most extraordinary successes could have countered the dissatisfaction with me. (*MD*, p. 179)

The problem for the daughter who is honorary son cannot be fully resolved. In imitating her father and benefiting from his attentions, she may also be rejecting what her mother seems to represent. In de Beauvoir's case, her father ultimately wanted her to follow a conventional female future, appropriate to his class. When he could not provide it, he wanted her to be an outstanding success. De Beauvoir did indeed achieve outstanding success at university. Years later, after the women's liberation movement, she said that up to then she had operated as a 'token woman', separated from solidarity with women and their experience. Her adolescence had also been marked by a gradual rejection of her mother with whom she did not wish to identify. It has been suggested (Evans, 1980) that her extreme ambivalence towards her mother explains de Beauvoir's overpowering feelings over her death. Whereas her father's death is dismissed in a line or so in her later autobiography, an entire book is devoted by de Beauvoir to that of her mother (*VED*).

I would also suggest that the father gradually ceased to be central to de Beauvoir after his rejection of her, and once Sartre had replaced the father as her intellectual mentor. Already, aged fifteen, she had imagined she would fall in love 'the day when a man would subjugate' her by his 'intelligence, culture and authority' (*MJF*, p. 145). (In 1961 I put a query in the margin; her feminism seemed to be in question.) She would not marry unless she encounterd someone 'more accomplished' than herself, although her 'equal' and 'double'. De Beauvoir, the adult writer, hastens to deny she was seeking a father replacement, because she sought independence and her own livelihood. 'Yet, the idea that I entertained of our couple was indirectly influenced by the feelings which I had held towards my father' (*MJF*, p. 146). Everything in her background had shown her that women were 'an inferior caste' which 'paternal prestige' confirmed. Since men had greater privileges, she could only recognise a man as her equal if he 'surpassed' her. (Again, I showed youthful scepticism in the margin.) There is a paternal tone in Sartre's declaration: 'From now on, I'm going to take you under my wing' (*MD*, p. 339), which de Beauvoir quotes uncritically. It is no coincidence that de Beauvoir dates her longings for a companion back to an adolescent turning point:

Sartre conformed exactly to the wishes I had entertained from the age of fifteen: he was the double in whom I found all my manic enthusiasms.' (*MJF*, p. 344)

• Mother: identification or exile

To describe the paternal influence on the young Simone is not to deny her experience and identity as female. De Beauvoir has fully documented the added constraints put upon her precisely because she was a girl. There were competing influences in her childhood. The young Simone was formed also by external schooling and other influences in which both parents collaborated. Her working-class nanny Louise also gave fleeting glimpses of an alternative perspective. But her contact with the 'real destitution' in which Louise later lived did not make her question the social order (*MD*, p. 131). Although the young Simone did not sense herself inferior when comparing herself with boys, in the realm of adults she did notice the distinction:

In certain respects, Papa, grandpa and my uncles appeared to me to be superior to their wives. But in my everyday life, it was Louise, Mama, grandmama and my aunts who played the leading roles. (*MD*, p. 55)

Simone's mother and other female figures were charged with her moral and spiritual welfare. The young girl was subject to their continuous intervention in the minutiae of daily life. The mother was the supreme petty controller, whereas her father raised her up 'to his level'. When she returned to her 'ordinary level', she was dependent on her mother; 'Papa had allowed her to take complete charge of my bodily and moral welfare' (*MD*, p. 37);

Her hold over me actually derived in large part from our intimacy. My father treated me like a fully grown person, my mother took care of the child that I was. (*MJF*, pp. 41–2)

The delegation to women of the task of policing women for subordination is a common practice. The young Simone was obliged to learn in one dramatic incident that the father would not tolerate a child criticising the mother. Papa declared: 'A child who sets up as a judge of his mother is an imbecile' (*MD*, p. 108). The young daughter blushed scarlet and left the room.

The contrast between Simone's upbringing and that of her cousin Jacques reveals the constraints put upon Simone as female. Although she was encouraged to read, books were censored by her mother, who clipped together certain pages and trusted her not to open them. Both Simone and her friend Zaza had their letters opened and read by their mothers. By contrast, Jacques could read whatever he fancied. Simone looked up to Jacques' wider knowledge of exciting writers. Jacques had freedom of movement in the streets and cafés, Simone was greatly confined. In her teens she and her sister broke free to explore secretly the world of the Paris bars. They were to learn the limits of this freedom when Simone escaped attack by several young men who demanded that her openness be expressed in sexual terms (*MD*, p. 274). By contrast, Jacques could with impunity indulge in adventures, sexual or otherwise, according to choice.

The *Memoirs* also document some of the contrasts and similarities in the upbringing of Simone's great friend Zaza, who was subject to more severe constraints, including a rigid adherence to a system of arranged marriages. She was given far less time for reading and had to spend hours preparing elaborate meals. She had less solitude than Simone, whose mother permitted her greater freedom in 'the more important things'. Simone's mother did not interfere with her work and choice of friends and demanded minimum help around the house. Simone was asked to do only the sort of tasks habitually expected of boys, like emptying the rubbish. That same minimum involvement in domestic work was to continue into adulthood.

In another sense, the mother's intervention was profound and not amenable to change by intellectual effort. Maman policed her daughter's body; this was not extraordinary, simply the transmission of values to which the mother had herself been subjected in childhood, and which de Beauvoir, expanding on suggestions already in the *Memoirs*, describes with brutal clarity after her mother's death. Her mother, she writes:

lived against herself. She had appetites in plenty; she spent all her strength in repressing them and she underwent this denial in anger. In her childhood her body, her heart and her mind had been squeezed into an armour of principles and prohibitions. She had been taught to pull the laces hard and tight herself. A full blooded, spirited woman lived on inside her, but a stranger to herself, deformed and mutilated. (*VED*, p. 38)

The transmission of these values was different for each daughter. Here de Beauvoir unusually offers an interpretation with psychoanalytical overtones. As above, the interpretation is offered several years after the mother's death. De Beauvoir suggests that because her mother had been jealous of her own father's preference for her younger sister Lili, Madame de Beauvoir in turn identified with Simone the elder. She also ascribed to Simone 'the loftiest intellectual and moral qualities' (*VED*, p. 29). Her mother also helped with her homework. She even learned English and Latin in order to assist her school progress (*MD*, p. 38). Simone was thus given intellectual support by both mother and father, the one concentrated on schoolwork, the other on studies outside. Her sister escaped the negative effects of the extreme surveillance imposed upon Simone, who had been 'frozen' at a very early age by her mother's 'prudishness' (*VED*, p. 59). Poupette 'had been less marked by Maman, and so she had not inherited her stiffness; and she had a freer relationship with her' (*ibid.*, p. 61).

The *Memoirs* document most fully Simone's own experience and emerging attitudes towards sexuality. As in the case of other girls of that epoch, the repression of sexuality was legitimated by religion, which in turn was intertwined with maternal piety and authority. Maman de Beauvoir 'was apt to confuse sexuality with vice: she always associated fleshly desire with sin' (*MD*, p. 38):

At every instant, even in the secret of my heart, she was my witness and I rarely made a distinction between her gaze and that of God. (*MJF*, p. 41)

The young Simone could see that her mother was no saint, but that made her even more powerful as an example to follow.

She was duty bound 'to equal her in piety and virtue' (*MJF*, p. 41):

> without striving to imitate her, I was moulded by her. She inculcated in me a sense of duty . . . My father was not averse to putting himself forward, but I learnt from Mama to efface myself, to censor my desires, to say and do exactly what ought to be said and done. I demanded nothing and I dared little. (*MJF*, p. 43)

Here, then, the young Simone did not imitate the bravado of her father but instead saw her mother as the one to imitate.

When the young Simone stopped believing in God, partly because she realised that he did not influence her conduct, her belief in a moral law remained 'deeply engraved' in her. De Beauvoir's respect for her mother 'gave a sacred character to her decrees'. So she continued to 'submit' to them. 'Ideas of duty, merit, sexual taboos: all were retained' (*MJF*, p. 139). That single sentence I once underlined. The maternal influence was for Simone all pervasive, long after its religious impetus was eroded; mother's moral law itself became sacred.

One such sexual taboo was that she should never look at herself naked; she was obliged to change her underwear without uncovering herself. 'In my universe, the flesh had no right to existence. Yet, I had known the sweetness of maternal arms' (*MJF*, p. 60). Here de Beauvoir recognises the paradox of prudery imposed by women who simultaneously have sensual rapport with their infants. My ink marks also somehow recognised this.

The lessons of the body cannot so easily be unlearned, the body can be seen to have 'a memory' of a non-verbal kind (Bourdieu, 1977, p. 94). De Beauvoir describes how she was discouraged from physical activities like swimming or bicycling; even ballroom dancing lessons made her feel inhibited: 'Nudity was for me confused with indecency' (*MJF*, p. 163). In her milieu no frankness about bodily functions ever broke through the conventions. She confesses that in her early teens sexuality frightened her (*ibid.*, p. 163), and such views could not be discarded simply by an intellectual change of mind. Recalling the adolescent escapades which she and her sister had in bars and dance halls, she is overcome with a 'virtuous revulsion'. 'Despite my rationalism, the things of the flesh remained taboo for me' (*MJF*, p. 289).

De Beauvoir's relationship with her mother was as problematic as that with her father. Recently, feminists have begun to re-examine orthodox psychoanalysts' accounts of the emergence of individual identity (Chodorow, 1978; Gardiner, 1982). A male, usually nurtured by a female, attains his gender identity in negative fashion by learning he is not female. He gains autonomy by outgrowing the mother-child symbiosis and identifying with the father. The female, by contrast, 'forms her gender identity positively by becoming like the mother with whom she begins life in a symbiotic merger' (Gardiner, 1982, p. 182). Her identity, unlike the boy's, is not a progressive and sudden break with the female nurturer; she has to learn to be separate, but knows that in adulthood she is ideally to become a wife and mother. Theorists of male identity emphasise developmental *progress* whereas theorists of female identity emphasise *process* (*ibid.*, p. 182). Chodorow sees female identity as cyclical, relational and fluid (1978).

A young girl who sees her mother as victim and subordinate to her father, who has the symbolic power of the phallus may seek to reject identification with the mother. She will, however, have problems separating the negative aspects of her mother from those which she admires. A psychoanalytical perspective empha-sises the girl's ambivalence in terms of an infant's early split between the 'good' and 'bad' mother. Others, such as Chodorow, put greater emphasis on later roles, where the mother is seen as socially subordinate. In either case there is ambivalence in the daughter.

Something of this mother-daughter relationship, Gardiner suggests, has been explored in recent women's fiction where 'the most disturbing villain is not the selfish or oppressive male but instead the bad mother'. This mother-villain is so frightening 'because she is what the daughter fears to become and what her infantile identifications predispose her to become' (1982, p. 186). The author may resolve this fear by making the mother utterly repulsive or by killing her off in the text. This fear is also discussed by Adrienne Rich:

Matrophobia can be seen as a womanly splitting of the self, in the desire to become purged once and for all of our mother's bondage, to become individuated and free. The mother stands for the victim in ourselves, the unfree woman, the martyr. (1977, p. 236)

De Beauvoir's *Memoirs* are an intriguing testimony of the conflicting pressures in the young Simone's search for identity. Encouraged by her father to imitate his intellectual interests, she could not progress as a male to become like him, thereby rejecting the female identity exemplified by her mother. Indeed her father actually rejected *her* at puberty. From early childhood, while anger was directed at seemingly female characteristics, many of the male characteristics which she attributed to her father and to other males seemed utterly alluring and were to remain so through adulthood. In the *Memoirs* her image of the male world verges on fantasy. When she walked past her cousin's college she:

conjured up the mystery which was being celebrated behind those walls: a classroom of boys, and I felt myself in exile. They had as teachers, brilliant, intelligent men who conveyed to them knowledge in its full splendour. My old schoolmistresses only communicated it to me in expurgated, insipid and faded form. They nourished me with ersatz and I was kept in a cage. (*MJF*, p. 123)

This male feast of knowledge, likened to the celebration of a mystery, has the overtones of a holy communion. By contrast, her female teachers 'nourish' her with only a substitute for the pure blood of the male saviour, the soured milk of infancy which she wishes to outgrow. She did not entirely despair, but consoled herself in a confident future: 'either through learning or talent, some women had carved their place in the universe of men' (*MJF*, p. 123). These few words of consolation I once underlined. Like her, it did not seem possible to transform the dominant universe: women could enter it only as alien individuals. I also identified with her impatience at 'insipid and faded' learning from my teachers (see also Okely, 1978).

In despising the pettiness of her mainly female teachers, the young Simone did not see that they were merely delegates in a system approved by absent men. She learned also to associate moral and sexual controls with a 'punishing' and 'bad' mother, although her father, with equal conviction, wished them on his daughters. In the desire to disassociate herself from the 'bad' or victim mother, she risked simultaneously rejecting the positive aspects of womanhood.

Mary Evans has suggested that for de Beauvoir, the father represented reason whereas the mother symbolised at an unconscious level powerful emotional forces 'that she had to exclude, or place on a rational level, in her own life' (1985, p. 55). De Beauvoir was left with extreme ambivalence towards her mother. Her anger at the bodily, sexual constraints in women's upbringing, so vividly denounced in *The Second Sex*, was also anger at her own upbringing under her mother's direct tutelage. The writing of the *Memoirs* in her mother's lifetime brought guilt, and de Beauvoir asked her sister to mediate. When her mother died, and in contrast to her father's death, grief engulfed her. Perhaps this was guilt for having 'killed her off' long ago in life.

The rejection of what her mother represented could never be permanently achieved. In her mother's death, de Beauvoir unexpectedly found a major aspect with which she could identify, namely her mother's resistance to death. Her mother also got rid of 'the ready-made notions that hid her sincere and lovable side' (*VED*, p. 91). De Beauvoir gradually ceased to separate the 'darling Maman' she had loved when ten years old and the 'inimical woman' who had 'oppressed' her adolescence (*ibid.*, p. 89). It seemed temporarily possible to identify with the 'good' mother again. In mourning, she became her mother, the person she had striven not to imitate. Sartre told de Beauvoir that her mouth was no longer her own; it moved like that of her mother.

One radical feminist line classifies women as either 'male identified' or 'woman identified'. The latter has 'fought patriarchal conditioning so that she values herself and is loyal to other women' (Gardiner, 1982, p. 184). The former is 'a term of abuse applied to other women who cast their "social, political, and intellectual allegiances with men"' (Rich and Gardiner 1982, p. 184). Yet the split is not so simple. If de Beauvoir had aligned herself to many of the values conveyed by her mother and teachers, she would also in effect have been aligning herself with the hidden patriarch. Moreover, she grew up to reject her father's political beliefs — his nationalism and racism, as well as his support for a class hierarchy, the family and women's dependency. Her intellectual training was turned around to subvert the content of her father's beliefs, not just those of her mother. In this sense it is also inadequate to suggest (see Walters, 1976; Evans, 1985) that de Beauvoir's youthful struggle was merely an imitation of the petty bourgeoisie to which her family was relegated and which emphasised individual achievement. De Beauvoir defied both the gender divisions and the political ideology of her class.

● Space, gender and nature

Among the significant differences in female and male experience in a sexist society is freedom of movement beyond domestic space. The image of confinement is recurrent in women's writing (Gardiner, 1982, p. 178). The woman's body has itself been subjected in many cultures to greater restrictions than men (see Okely, 1978). De Beauvoir uses the image of corsetry as metaphor and fact to describe her mother's upbringing, part of which was passed on. Simone's mother and others curbed the young girl's spontaneity, imposed a sense of bodily shame, and controlled her bodily movements (*VED*, p.34). These experiences in de Beauvoir's childhood heightened her generalised view of women's constraints on movement. For example, in *The Second Sex*, de Beauvoir identifies with Marie Bashkirtsev's lament that she cannot walk alone: the need always to be accompanied makes the 'wings drop'. De Beauvoir complains that the requirement for a woman constantly to be aware of her appearance and deportment 'rivets her to the ground'. She contrasts this with the experience of the eighteen-year-old T. E. Lawrence who made an extended journey through France alone on a bicycle. There is anger, if not envy, when she states that a girl would not be able to do the same, much less cross the desert, as Lawrence did a year later. 'Such experiences have incalculable import: it is then that the individual intoxicated by freedom and discovery learns to regard the entire earth as his fief' (*DS* I, p. 556, omitted by Parshley).

An urban environment such as Paris need not necessarily be a reason for confinement, but for girls in particular it can be defined as a place of danger. Earlier another French woman writer, George Sand, when young, gained the freedom of walking the

Paris streets only by disguising herself in boy's clothes. Simone was herself confined. She was fascinated to watch the passersby from the dining-room balcony when the family lived in the boulevard Raspail. To her distress, when they moved to the fifth floor on rue de Rennes she could no longer watch the people. She felt cut off from the world. In the country, isolation did not matter, nature overpowered her, whereas 'the essence of a city is in its inhabitants . . . Already I was beginning to want to escape from the narrow circle in which I was confined' (*MD*, p. 55).

Part of her escape was to travel in the mind. Studying in her armchair, she listened to the 'harmony of the spheres' (*MJF*, p. 69). Impatient over petty tasks, she preferred 'to call up the past, illuminate the five continents, descend to the centre of the earth and encircle the moon' (*ibid.*, p. 70). When she opened her English books, she felt that she was 'leaving on a journey' (*ibid.*, p. 69). Books were a liberation from confinement in time and space; she even used the word *dépayser* (to change scenery or disorientate) to describe what they did for her: books displaced her from her known territory. It could of course be argued that boys also imagine and read of exciting, exotic adventures. A genre of schoolboy literature confirms this. The difference is that males, especially those of a privileged class, can more easily see their childhood as an apprenticeship for possibilities of adult exploration.

Another escape from home confinement for the young Simone, in this case not symbolic but an authentic expansion in physical space, was her summer vacations at her grandparents' home. Here she was allowed freer range, and outdoors her body could give way to sensuality in the summer heat. Her happiness then reached its 'apogee'. The metaphor is spatial – interplanetary indeed. Without a strict timetable, with diminished control by adults, she describes also how she enjoyed greater leisure to read and to play with her sister. She also welcomed greater attention from her father and the more relaxed mood of her mother in this setting. She revelled in 'la solitude, la liberté' (*MJF*, p. 76). These words I once underlined, recognising also the longed-for freedom found in solitude in a rural landscape. De Beauvoir moves in the text from an account of the controls and pettiness of her schoolteachers to the contrasting countryside. When the history teacher decides to punish her by separating her from Zaza, de Beauvoir recalls the confined location: 'in that sad corridor' she realises that her childhood has moved to another stage:

I no longer ruled over the world; the façades of buildings and *indifferent looks of passers by exiled me*. That is why my love of the countryside took on mystical colours. As soon as I arrived at Meyrignac, the ramparts crumbled, the horizon retreated. *I lost myself in the infinite all the while remaining myself* . . . the wind whirled around the poplars; it came from elsewhere, from everywhere, it turned space around and I swirled, immobile, right to the ends of the earth. (*MJF*, p. 126, my youthful emphasis)

When the moon rose, she 'communicated with cities, deserts, seas and villages . . . I was no longer a vacant consciousness, an abstract gaze.' She became the very smells and heat of her surroundings. She felt heavy yet she was also as light as air. 'I no longer had boundaries' (*ibid.*, p. 126). Supremely she loses all sense of bodily and spatial confines. While sometimes choosing to remain fixed, she is yet free to become one with the movement and elements of nature. Simone would stay outdoors as long as possible, hating a return to 'the enclosed space and adults' sclerotic time' (*MJF*, p. 127). Similarly the return to Paris was associated with a return to control by adults. In adolescence she found temporary release in 'the poetry of the bars', until she learned the boundaries imposed by males, and when shame and a work ethic returned.

In her early years, the young Simone associates the elation experienced in the countryside with the presence of God. She gives this an egoistic twist; since God was only spirit, her body had to be the intermediary to know the sensual qualities of, for instance, the sun or dew. Her presence was necessary to make nature come to life. In this she was charged with a mission (*MJF*, p. 127). While ignoring de Beauvoir's references to God, I once responded to this certainty in individual destiny. Today I read the same text with dispassion and recognise instead the existentialist interpretation which she laid upon her childhood experience, namely the need for the individual presence to bring the objective world to life.

The countryside and her vision there of nature was both a freedom in space and a sensual awakening. The body was divested of its controls and she projected her longings on to nature, seemingly uncontrolled. The countryside was the site for eroticism and autonomy. As she began to acquire greater freedom from adult control, the countryside no longer carried the same meaning. The break came with the death of her grandfather and the transfer of the country property. Her visits would eventually cease; she was ready for something else. On her return in mourning attire to Paris, she describes a hitherto absent sensual awareness which is now projected on to the city chestnut blossom and even the hot tarmac (*MJF*, pp. 319–20). Sensuality had different implications once de Beauvoir experienced it through and with another person rather than in the autonomy of virginity. Her heterosexual experience of sexuality was to carry the pain of jealousy; she had lost the solitude of virgin sexuality. Henceforth in adulthood, 'nature' whether as the biology of pregnancy or her view of the countryside was seen as a source of weakness and immanence.

This split view of nature – either as a source of sensual freedom and autonomy or as a mysterious diversion to be overpowered – continues throughout her work. In Volume I of *The Second Sex* when exposing the myths attached to woman or when inveighing against the physical burdens of pregnancy, de Beauvoir sees the links between nature and woman as a dangerous rationale for women's subordination. Volume II, by contrast, recreates her childhood experience of nature and the countryside as sensual and spatial release.

In the adult autobiographies, nature has become something to conquer, and Paris the urban space remained her self-made home once it was freed from a sense of enclosure created by others. However, de Beauvoir's need to move freely and far has been continuous. Her adult hill walks and a 'frenetic' desire to travel are consistent with a defiance of past feminine confinement (see Chapter 5).

My virginal reading of the *Memoirs* shared de Beauvoir's sense of freedom for the body in nature. In my case, nature was seen to defy especially the institutional controls of school (see Okely, 1978). Summer holidays out of London were also savoured.

Unlike de Beauvoir, the urban metropolis, Paris, was the site for a new autonomy. Since I came there as a stranger, I could make my own timetable, governed only by self-selected lectures at the Sorbonne. True, the whole of France, rural or urban, became a hitchhiker's territory, although never on my own. My friend Margaret and I saw the countryside and coast as a release from bodily constraints. We slept rough in a haystack or on the cliffs. We swam naked in the March Brittany sea. Sometimes mere mileage was proof of freedom. My sister and I hitchhiked through the Netherlands, and after I pinned up the maps with ink marks tracing our routes: our conquest of space. Free movement was to be impeded at times. Margaret and I had to leap out of a car when the driver suddenly left the main route. Once on a deserted beach, when a man threw me to the ground, Margaret jumped on his back, screamed and frightened him off. The countryside was thus also populated with menace.

Paris was my major base in which to strive for free movement. I wrote poems to the place. The restrictions now came from male strangers. Previously, rules to keep me 'within the bounds' came only from female authorities in school. Later, London did not compare with Paris, because it was familiar and, possibly, because I lived in a suburb. I wrote: 'the dust in Paris is ever whirling and sweeping in clouds – the dust of London creeps in, settles and stays. In London one again finds the complication of adaptation and tolerance.' Thus the urban space was seen to mirror either freedom or constraint, depending on my position.

Back in Paris in May 1961 I declared it a special haunt for 'reading, learning and discovery. The choice confronted and known in this place.' Already I had absorbed de Beauvoir's emphasis on individual choice. But a few days later I recorded the constraints on movement; the very constraints which de Beauvoir recognised in *The Second Sex*. After a comment on de Beauvoir, I noted:

How the masculine world crushes us. We are unable to walk alone down the street. I sometimes return in tears from my walks because I am tormented by people's commentaries, I walk about less often now. They, the men, want to encourage my self consciousness and narcissism. I am narcissistic. That is why I cover up my mirror with a black cloth. I hate finding myself absorbed in my own face. Mirrors for women. Oh hell what legacies for us. I cannot go anywhere, particularly in Paris, without being on guard.

A page later, when considering my turning away from the once longed-for artist, I associated a potential sexual partnership with both a compromise of freedom *and* a flight from sexual harassment in the streets:

I do not want to be accepted as un membre d'un couple. Until women are allowed to wander the earth alone and undisturbed by others they cannot create. They waste or use up their energies in fighting for freedom. It is damn easy to give in and settle down. It is bloody easy to take a lover and be normal. No wonder women have found artistic inspiration in Nature, there where they could project their ideals and images because they were unwatched and unfollowed. Soon I shall have to retire to a country retreat when they will leave me alone in my CHOSEN ABANDONMENT.

De Beauvoir's discussion of nature and freedom of movement had brought recognition and in turn affected the reader's interpretation of her experience.

This discussion of space, gender and nature reveals that physical space, whether urban or rural, is never neutral; it is socially shaped. Within the same place an individual's movement and experience will be affected by factors such as gender. In de Beauvoir's case, her use of rural space and nature can be seen as symbolic attempts, albeit illusory, to escape the dominant patriarchal culture where for a young girl, domestic space may be neither a peaceful retreat nor necessarily private, but instead a place of confinement and surveillance. (One of her joys in later acquiring a room of her own was the right to close the door behind her (*PL*).) Nature and the rural landscape which the Parisian schoolgirl visited only on vacation were experienced as culture-free. Her body was divested of some of its controls. In fact not even 'nature' is culture-free; if de Beauvoir had lived permanently in a rural area she would have been subjected to different constraints.

For her, it seemed, freedom was imaginable only outside society, and the freedom she attained was of a highly individualistic kind. De Beauvoir's youthful emancipation entailed cutting herself off from society and isolating herself from both women and men, except for the shared experience of nature with her friend Zaza. Even this her mother censored when she read of it in Simone's letter to Zaza. De Beauvoir's individual escape (like my own in Paris and France), whether in nature or an alien land, could only be an illusion. Her struggles for autonomy carry all the problems which a lone woman faces when seeking emancipated achievement without others and without a total transformation of the society she aspires to transcend.

CHAPTER THREE

THE IMPACT OF
The Second Sex

The Second Sex was first published in 1949 and translated into English in 1953. Its significance in the 1950s and 1960s for isolated middle-class western women was immense. In the 1970s it was used as a starting point in the women's movement and in consciousness-raising groups. It is read differently in the 1980s. Today, for a younger generation of feminists, it is criticised as pessimistic and without any clear direction for liberation. Yet we should not overlook its historical significance. People read from it what they wished. When first published it was seen as a monstrosity by the right and, to de Beauvoir's surprise, viewed with ambivalence or disfavour by the left (*F Ci*, pp. 200–1), for the communist line that the subordination of women would disappear after a socialist revolution paralleled de Beauvoir's concluding paragraphs. Moreover, both its supporters and its critics saw it as a manifesto. Elizabeth Hardwick described it as 'so briskly Utopian it fills one with a kind of shame and sadness, like coming upon manifestos and committee programmes in the attic' (1953).

De Beauvoir has said that she did not begin working on *The Second Sex* as a feminist. She had been intending to write some memoirs but 'wanting to talk about myself I became aware that to do so I should first have to describe the condition of women in general' (*F Ci*, p. 195). At the time she apparently believed that being a woman had made no difference in her life; it was Sartre who suggested that this could not be the case (*F Ci*, p. 103). This blindness towards gender is now recognised within the feminist movement as the standard experience of a 'token woman' within a male-dominated circle. The individual successful woman rarely experiences explicit, observable discrimination and rejection because she is safely incorporated without challenging the male monopoly (see *F Ci*, p. 189). De Beauvoir has subsequently recognised the trap of the token woman and warned against it (1976, p. 78).

De Beauvoir has said that she became a feminist only after the book was published, and 'above all after the book had lived for other women' (1978), from whom she received thousands of letters. Some said it changed their lives. 'If my book has helped women, it is because it expressed them, and they in turn gave it its truth' (*F Ci*, p. 203).

A subsequent generation of feminists and male sympathisers have found the book, just from the measure of their own contrasting experience, both false and depressing. They cannot recognise any authenticity because the historical conditions have changed. Women from other races and cultures have not, in any case, necessarily recognised their own experience in the text at any time. *The Second Sex*'s hope for transformation seems to rest partly on women's recognition of their own complicity in their subordination and only very vaguely on a socialist revolution which women must apparently await without any autonomous movement. Socialism is tacked on as an afterthought. It seems that women must wait for their male socialist liberator. Since the women's movement of the 1970s, de Beauvoir has publicly changed her position, declaring that women's liberation cannot wait upon socialism and some male liberator. Instead the specific subordination of women should be acknowledged in an autonomous movement, although in conjunction with a class revolution (see 1972 interview in Schwarzer 1984).

It seems that the existentialist theory which underpinned the material was largely glossed over. The theoretical implications of de Beauvoir's existentialism are embedded in her descriptive material; they are hardly highlighted in a separate discussion. De Beauvoir does not, for example, explain in the book the specific development which her theory makes in terms of Sartre's work. Consequently there is little evidence that the thousands of women readers of *The Second Sex* interpreted it in relation to Sartre's early philosophical work, let alone that of Hegel. The detailed existentialist implications were ignored, or only half understood.

The section on myths was the initial stimulus for writing the book. She first considered the myths which men had created about women in their 'cosmologies, religion, superstitions, ideologies and literature' (*F Ci*, p. 195). It was Sartre who suggested that she do some groundwork in physiology or biology and she was convinced that both this and history would be necessary in order not to leave the myths 'hanging in mid-air' without conveying 'the reality those myths were intended to mask' (*ibid.*, p. 195). In fact, her caricature of a Marxist or materialist explanation still leaves the myths ungrounded. Although de Beauvoir rests her major explanation for women's subordination on the existentialist assertion that they were seen as 'Other' by males, she explains this, despite herself, partly in terms of biology:

From humanity's beginnings, their biological advantage has enabled the males to affirm their status as sole and sovereign subjects, they have never abdicated this position . . . Condemned to play the part of the Other, woman was also condemned to hold only uncertain power: slave or idol, it was never she who chose her lot. (*2nd S*, p. 109)

The general invisibility of existentialist theory was ensured by another crucial factor in the English translation of *The Second Sex* in 1953. The translator selected was a Professor of Zoology, Howard Parshley, who sanitised and mistranslated a great deal of the existentialist terminology. Ten per cent of the book has been cut. Half the chapter on history and the names of more than seventy women in history have been expunged. In his introduction we are misled as follows:

I have also done some cutting and condensation here and there with a view to brevity, chiefly in reducing the extent of the author's illustrative material, especially in certain of her quotations from other writers. Practically all such modifications have been made with the author's express permission, passage by passage. (1972, pp. 11–12)

Margaret Simons (1983) has drawn attention to the cuts in the history chapter and the large missing sections on housework; the deletion of lesbian poetry, and the arbitrary choice of words for Marxist and existentialist terminology. For example:

de Beauvoir's regular use of the Marxist concept mystification is variously translated as 'hoax', 'mockery' or 'mystification'. The Hegelian term alienation – important for both Marxism and existentialism – is inconsistently translated as 'projection' or 'identification'. (1983, p. 563)

This mistranslation undermines de Beauvoir's claim that her thesis 'owed so much to Marxism and showed it in such a favourable light' (*F Ci*, p. 200). De Beauvoir has only recently noticed the extent of the changes and has expressed profound disappointment in a letter to Simons.

The zoologist translator has also highlighted some of her stray asides as introductory sentences to new paragraphs. He has broken up her text in ways which are consistent with his view rather than with de Beauvoir's. Key concepts from existentialism, Marxism and from psychoanalysis are made banal. The lyrical rhythm of her polemic is lost. Some of the English phrases and sentences are so clumsy they are almost unreadable. Many critical comments on American society have been laundered out, especially in the discussion of myths.[1] The translator was working at the text during the McCarthy era: presumably any critique of American myths was deemed inappropriate.

I have scrupulously checked the significance of the mistranslations and will draw attention to their implications. Where necessary I have made my own translation. A close and detailed scrutiny of the original French is required today: we have to know whether it is de Beauvoir or Parshley who is being criticised.

The Second Sex is a remarkable multi-disciplined undertaking which few intellectuals and academics would repeat today. Specialists in such subjects as history, literary criticism, political economy, philosophy and anthropology would hardly dare stray beyond their own expertise when studying women or gender. Not only are the social sciences more demarcated as separate disciplines – for example, sociology, economics and psychology – but they also have their own sub-specialisms. There are both historians and sociologists whose work is devoted almost entirely to the subject of women (for example, Rowbotham and Oakley). Back in the 1940s, de Beauvoir set herself the task of a Renaissance woman, covering an enormous range of disciplines in order to present an overview of women's condition and an explanation for their subordination.

The mass of intriguing material which she unearthed is organised around some key themes, although it is often difficult to recognise them and in some instances her argument is contradictory. The documentary evidence has since been overtaken in many areas, but at the time of the book's publication its breadth forced the reader to examine the facts and implication of women's subordination in every nook and cranny.

That women are subordinate is stated without compromise: 'From the time history began they have always been subordinate to man' (*DS*I, p. 18). De Beauvoir looks at a number of alternative explanations for this in biology, psychology and economics, and concludes that none of these approaches is sufficient. Evidence for the subordination of women is then examined through the documentation and interpretation of history in a chronology from the earliest hunter-gatherer societies to agriculturalists, from classical antiquity through to modern European and specifically French history.

This factual investigation is followed by an analysis of ideology, namely the myths associated with women and the 'feminine'. Religions, rituals, mythology and literature from around the world are scrutinised for representations of 'woman'. De Beauvoir suggests that there are similarities across cultures, and that in all cases women are idealised or debased in fantasy and misrepresentations which both reflect and reinforce women's actual subordination. The mystification of women is then more closely studied in the literary representations of five male authors, only one of whom, according to de Beauvoir, offers anything which approximates a plausible portrayal of women as human beings in their own right.

The concern with the concrete experience of women, in contrast to their misrepresentation, is pursued in Volume II. There are detailed accounts of women's existence from birth to old age, showing how, from childhood, women are made feminine, not born so. The description of different categories, for example the wife, mother, prostitute and mystic, explores the limited possibilities open to women and discusses the idea of the independent woman. In conclusion, de Beauvoir offers no programme for change except the inevitable emancipation of women with the advent of socialism.

The organising theory which underpins *The Second Sex* is drawn from the existentialism of Sartre and the philosophy of Hegel. In this book there is not the space to analyse in detail the extent to which de Beauvoir has adopted or modified some of their concepts. Some work has been done on aspects of Hegel's influence (see Craig, 1979), and work (by Moi) is in progress on the ways in which de Beauvoir replicated or modified Sartre's specific view of sexuality and the body in his *Being and Nothingness* (1943). Ultimately the strength of *The Second Sex* does not lie in de Beauvoir's refinements of abstract philosophy, except that her crucial focus on gender challenged any tendency in philosophers to make pronouncements about a gender-free 'man'.

The existentialist implications of de Beauvoir's arguments are briefly outlined as follows. Existentialism challenges any notion of a universal and fixed 'human nature'. Human beings create themselves in specific and changing situations. Maximum emphasis is placed on the freedom of the individual to choose his or her existence. A person's being is revealed by reflection on his or her unique concrete situation in time and space; it cannot be understood objectively and in the abstract. Minimum emphasis is placed on external determining factors which would limit the individual's choice. Thus the influence of the social, economic and historical context is underplayed. Similarly, other factors such as class and ethnic position are not extensively explored, although Sartre later gave greater representations to external factors as he engaged more fully with Marxism. An extreme view of existentialist choice would be that at each given moment individuals have the freedom to create themselves anew and to alter even seemingly fixed aspects of their past. No one has a predetermined position, so each individual is in a state of anxiety, faced with a terrifying aloneness and the responsibility of freedom. The individual should recognise that he or she has chosen either to confront or to avoid the making of choices. People are guilty of self-deception or 'bad faith' if they fail to grasp their own radical freedom.

True freedom is attained in moving from an inert or fixed state of 'immanence' towards the ideal of 'transcendence' through action. To transcend him or herself the individual should engage in projects in the world. Sartre distinguishes two types of being: that of *en-soi* (in-itself) and *pour-soi* (for-itself). Being-in-itself corresponds to the state of 'immanence' and can be compared to a fixed object which has a relationship neither with itself nor with anything outside. By contrast, being-for-itself represents a fluid, changeable state of being. An individual who acts and lives this way can move from immanence to transcendence.

Every individual is in a potentially dangerous struggle with others in the assertion of freedom. Since nothing is decided in advance, it cannot be predicted who will emerge triumphant. The notion of struggle was drawn from Hegel's master-slave dialectic. In his later work, Sartre was more affected by Marxism in recognising that individuals need not necessarily engage in competitive struggle, but instead seek solidarity with each other. The individual is threatened by the weight of others' freedom but also needs interaction with others in order to affirm his or her existence. The individual necessarily uses 'the other' for self-definition. He or she needs the other's gaze and presence as a confirmation of existence.

In *The Second Sex*, de Beauvoir refines the existentialist denial of any fixed 'human nature' by asserting that there is no fixed 'feminine nature'; it too is a creation. Similarly de Beauvoir minimises any determining influences from biology, economics, psychoanalysis and the unconscious. Neither does she explore the implications of class and race. She does however introduce a gender twist to the notion of struggle and to human beings' use of 'the Other' by suggesting that woman is *always* treated as 'the Other'. Woman never won the struggle, she is never the definer, never the subject in a mutual exchange, just the object.

Of the three types of external or 'objective' explanations for women's subordination, de Beauvoir devotes maximum space to biology. She states that so-called 'feminine' characteristics are neither dictated by hormones nor determined in parts of the brain. The biological differences are not sufficient to explain male domination. Women's exile from the world of men is not based in nature. Women's subordination was established at the outset when man presented himself as the 'essential' being and excluded woman from his system of thought and his projects in the world. Woman accepted this situation, which was later reinforced by education from generation to generation.

It is not clear why men first defined themselves as dominant. Muscular strength is an inadequate explanation since many societies condemn violence. But woman's 'enslavement' to the human species was an important factor. Whereas there is no conflict within a man's existence as an autonomous individual, a woman's existence as an autonomous individual is in conflict with the continuation of the species since she has to reproduce it through her body. Woman is thus weighed down by the reproductive demands of her body. She is engaged in a struggle between herself and the species. A man does not have to suffer such handicaps. Man therefore reduced woman to a reproductive object.

Nonetheless, the reproductive role is not sufficient to explain women's dependence. It is because men have *classified* women as Other and then reinforced this idea through institutions, laws and myths that women's subordination is continuous. De Beauvoir also rejects psychoanalytical and economic explanations in terms which minimise external factors and which again emphasise the ideological mechanism of man treating woman as 'Other'.

The notions of 'immanence' and 'transcendence' recur throughout her analysis. Women are seen to be trapped in immanence and men are engaged in transcendent projects. The extent to which women choose immanence is a matter of debate and is not always clarified by de Beauvoir. On the one hand, *The Second Sex* is a devastating account of the conditions of women's subordination which arise mainly from being treated as 'the Other' by man. On the other hand, de Beauvoir every now and then suggests that women collude with their subservient state; they do not confront their freedom to change. Throughout *The Second Sex* there is thus a continuing oscillation in the argument; women are weighed down by the weight of history, by their education and even by their reproductive role, yet they have chosen to remain 'beings-in-themselves' rather than acting to change as 'beings-for-themselves'. De Beauvoir's women readers faced a similar dilemma.

In her historical account de Beauvoir attempts to demonstrate the various ways in which woman has been 'immanent' and 'Other' in law and in practice. Although there are considerable inaccuracies in this massive overview, de Beauvoir should be credited with interrogating history from what was then a highly original perspective.

The analysis of myths exposed the most powerful and concentrated forms in which women have been seen as Other, as object and not subject. A major myth credits the male with creativity, while woman is mere earth or nature to his cultural plough. Myths about women are frequently shown to be bound up with a dangerous sexuality; de Beauvoir suggests that universally menstruation, virginity, defloration, pregnancy and childbirth are surrounded by strange 'taboos'. The woman is seen as disgusting flesh while apparently the man is not. De Beauvoir's intention is to de-mystify. Again there is an oscillation in her argument. On the one hand, there is the suggestion that there is no innate reason why women should be victims of these misrepresentations, on the other hand, she considers that aspects of female reproductive and bodily functions automatically explain why all men and societies apparently imagine and define women in a similar fashion.

The second volume, entitled 'L'Expérience Vécue' or 'Lived Experience', is held together by the existentialist emphasis on subjective experience. An individual cannot know about the world in objective fashion, but only through awareness of his or her own situation. De Beauvoir attempts to recreate the situation of women through the different stages of their lives and from the perspective of their inner feelings and responses.

A major theme is that woman is made, not born. There is a tension in the text between a brutal description of women's subordination as a social fact and a description of women's response to these conditions. Women are frequently seen to collaborate in their loss of freedom and are therefore guilty of bad faith. However, their subordination is never complete. Women seek to reassert themselves in devious ways. Some women over-react to their oppression by justifying it and acting out its extremes; for example, the narcissist who loves herself finds reality in the immanence of her own person. Some women treat love as a full-time occupation, just as the mystic also makes a fetish of love, although this time it is directed towards the divine.

Generally, women are depicted as resigned to their conditions and even as a reactionary force. Men help to maintain women's servitude and, in passing, de Beauvoir acknowledges that the situation of working-class men is hardly more enviable. They are also locked in immanence and suffer alienation in their work. Ultimately, only a collective awareness or raised consciousness will permit women to change their circumstances. Women should understand that there is no fixed feminine condition.

Minor changes here and there are inadequate for the necessary total transformation of society. Women with external jobs, for instance, merely return to the second job of domestic labour at home. The anti-feminists have claimed that women lack the qualities of genius, but if there have been few 'great' women artists, this is because woman's situation limits her experience. Economic independence is vital and that can only be achieved under socialism.

The underlying existentialist arguments in *The Second Sex* are only one aspect. The presentation of material from history, literature, biology, psychology and many other sources, all concerned with a single subject, has a cumulative impact. The polemic and value judgements challenged any suggestion that facts are objective and politically neutral. Some topics proved especially provocative in de Beauvoir's overview, including marriage, sex and maternity. So that the reader can get a flavour of her argument, I have summarised with minimum comment de Beauvoir's treatment of these topics in Volume II.

De Beauvoir's words encouraged a number of her women readers, including myself, to reject marriage. In the absence of co-operative childcare, both within and outside marriage, many of us also rejected or delayed maternity. Insofar as de Beauvoir gives a description of the bourgeois institution of marriage which presupposes the woman's position as that of economic dependant who offers unpaid services such as housework, sex, emotional support and major childcare, the text stands the test of time. The passages on this subject which I once underlined are, for the most part, still relevant. There have been some changes for middle-class western women. The married 'career' woman has avoided problems of an earlier generation by employing a working-class 'nanny' for childcare and domestic labour. Her economic dependence has thus been eased by the labour of other women. Similarly, certain middle-class women in the Third World are able to combine marriage and motherhood with a 'career'. The situation for the working-class woman with outside work, and that of the single mother, requires more concrete analysis than that once offered by de Beauvoir. Nevertheless, despite changes in sexual attitudes, birth control, legal reforms and divorce, marriage remains a dominant institution with continuing implications for the subordination of women. De Beauvoir's words retain their power.

Marriage

De Beauvoir discusses marriage as a bourgeois institution rather than as simply a personal relationship. The inequality between husband and wife is emphasised: whereas marriage is a woman's major identity and vocation, it is only a portion of a man's life. Whereas the woman is doomed to 'immanence' in this context, the man's work beyond the home and family offers the opportunity for transcendence. The woman is linked to the outside world only through the intermediary of her husband. The man 'takes' the woman and despite modifications in law she is still little more than his possession.

De Beauvoir is scathing about the notion of free choice among potential spouses. The woman needs marriage to obtain acceptance in society and is trained to direct her energies to trapping a husband. Without marriage, the woman in many groups is an outcast. Since the bourgeois woman is not educated to earn her own living, she knows that in order to maintain her class position she needs a husband because of his superior opportunities for earning a living.

Married love is a convenient invention for combining the institution of marriage with sexual needs. Just as in wider legal and political rights there is asymmetry in sexual rights and duties between husband and wife. The latter, at least in bourgeois circles, is required to enter marriage as a virgin. Indeed some middle-class women see marriage as a welcome relief from sexual repression. The husband is free to have both sex before marriage and extra-marital affairs, while a wife's adultery is subject to rigorous controls. The bride approaches the wedding bed with ambivalence. She is suddenly expected to be sensuous and abandon all previous restraint.

Even if the marriage is based on love, the institution will eventually kill it. Love should be reciprocal and spontaneous and founded on freedom. De Beauvoir suggests that sexual desire declines if a couple are united in 'transcendent' activities. Sexual union then becomes a form of mutual masturbation. (This curious assertion may speak more of her own relationships.) Marital sexuality risks becoming mechanical. At first mutual attraction is based on the notion of the partner being 'the Other' but after a while the partner becomes 'the same'. To sustain the sexual union, both partners resort to fantasies about other people.

Whereas sexual intercourse for a male coincides with orgasm it may not for a woman. So a married woman who is required to offer sexual services in part payment for economic support may never experience orgasm. Thus compulsory sex within marriage may be satisfying for a male but the very opposite for a female.

The wife is trapped within the home which is her prison. For men a home is not an end in itself. There are conflicting interests in the home for a husband and wife: for the one it is a 'springboard' to the outside world, for the wife it is the sole universe. De Beauvoir's discussion of the hearth and home derives mainly from observations of the bourgeoisie, and her analysis of housework inadvertently reflects the transition which European middle-class woman underwent after the Second World War. Less able to use domestic servants, the housewife experienced a form of proletarianisation. But even the pre-war woman with domestic servants is portrayed by de Beauvoir in a restricted world when supervising others. Housework can easily become obsessional, a sublimation for sexual frustration and an escape from the disillusionment of marriage. It is a flight from self-fulfilment.

De Beauvoir acknowledges that cooking and the purchase and preparation of food can be a creative activity, but even this has limited satisfaction. The division of work is such that the 'wife-servant' is charged with the 'inessential'. The living-place and meals are useful but do not themselves give meaning. The immediate household duties are not a real end; they are only anonymous projects. Domestic labour, she asserts, does not produce a lasting creative object. (This description is probably her most controversial, given the major analysis of domestic labour which came after the women's movement.) The housewife's work only makes sense if it is linked to society beyond: to production or action. Far from liberating the housewife, domestic labour puts her in a dependent position to her husband and children. She is never recognised as fulfilled, however much she is respected. She is 'subordinate, secondary and parasitic' (*DS* II, p. 247). Her life is defined essentially by the 'service' of the bed and the 'service' of housework.

The traditional honeymoon served to mask the crisis of transition for the woman. She is torn from normal life and then loses control of her fate. For evidence, de Beauvoir provides extensive quotes from psychologists and from women's diaries, including that of Sophie Tolstoy. But marriage can also be a crisis for a man. Both learn that they are isolated. Each spouse experiences marriage differently, partly because they do not share the same education and circumstance. Without mutual understanding, the newly married are in effect strangers.

Since marriage subordinates the wife to the husband, she is the one who experiences most acutely the contradictions in the relationship. One paradox lies in the combined social and erotic functions of marriage. On the one hand, the husband replaces the father as tutor and provider; he is a demi-god in whose shadow she must live. But on the other hand, the wife must share a sensual experience of which she has been brought up to be ashamed.

Various compromises are reached in the face of these contradictions. Often the husband is still seen as a respected superior whose 'animal weaknesses' are excused (*DS* II, pp. 256–7). The wife rarely confronts her ambivalent feelings towards her husband. By not doing so, she deceives herself; she remains in 'bad faith'. Even if she attempts to assert her independence, she is handicapped by her limited social position and lack of education. By contrast, the husband has the advantages of 'professional training', links with a political party and a trade union. 'Worker, citizen, his thought is engaged in action' (*DS* II, p. 259). The young woman is intellectually disadvantaged, not because of some difference in the brain, but because she is denied the opportunity to use her powers of reasoning. She is vulnerable to her husband's apparently superior logic, even if he is wrong. 'In masculine hands logic is often violence' (*ibid.*, p. 260). Faced with this, the young woman can resort only to silence, tears or to limited violence, like the smashing of china.

De Beauvoir explores the nuances of the psychic violence which a husband can inflict upon his spouse. He enjoys the role of mentor. The wife may leave it to the husband to forge common opinions on every subject and she becomes convinced of her own incapacity. Thus the institution of marriage encourages a 'capricious imperialism' in men. Yet the conquest is never complete. Although in theory the wife gives way to the husband's authority, in areas which deeply concern her she resists him, albeit covertly. She may absorb his political views but she holds fast to lessons of her upbringing, namely religion (*ibid.*, p. 263). (This very specific example clearly draws on de Beauvoir's memories of her own parents' contrasting opinions of religion.)

The wife may not succeed in contesting the husband's intellectual superiority, but she can take revenge by sexual manipulation. She may also try to belittle him: there are all sorts of tricks to which she may resort. She is trapped in a double bind. She both struggles with him to retain her autonomy but she also sets out to maintain a dependent position. She must work at keeping her husband by giving him neither too much nor too little freedom. She must beware of possible rivals, allowing him to 'cheat' a little with the odd mistress but not to find a replacement. This tradition of 'managing' a man, of continually pleasing him, is a 'sad science'. But she has no alternative; if he abandoned her, she would be helpless.

For there to be loyalty and friendship between spouses, the fundamental condition is that they should both be free in relation to each other and equal in practice. So long as the man alone possesses economic autonomy and that he holds, by law and custom, the privileges conferred by masculinity, it is natural that he should so often appear to be a tyrant, something which incites woman to revolt and to trickery. (*DS* II, pp. 269–70)

No one denies the existence of marital conflict, but de Beauvoir does not accept the explanation that the problems are caused by the faults of individuals. Instead she finds the explanation for conflicts in the institution itself. Even marriages which appear to work have achieved an unhappy equilibrium – the price is boredom or hypocrisy. The bourgeoisie, especially, have invented a grotesque form of deception: 'ennui becomes wisdom, family hatreds are the profoundest form of love' (*DS* II, p. 274).

Ideally, people should be linked to each other only by free recognition of their love. In this way, de Beauvoir occasionally intervenes with a positive and somewhat romantic or idealistic observation about the possibility of a free, open love between a man and a woman. This cannot, she says, be achieved in the present circumstances and so long as the woman is dependent. Even companionship and shared interests are limited, as, for example when a woman collaborates in the husband's work, without her own independent work. A wife who acts as transcriber, manuscript correcter and adviser in her husband's intellectual work is cruelly replaceable. Since the woman is totally dependent, she can know only an inner, abstract freedom.

Maternity and reproduction

Before discussing motherhood, de Beauvoir focuses on the control of reproduction. At the time of her writing, both contraception and abortion were illegal in Catholic countries. The covert but widespread practice of abortion, she suggests, exposes the hypocrisy of bourgeois society and the church. While the church authorises the killing of men in war, it is uncompromising about the foetus. While men universally forbid abortion, they cynically use it to solve their individual problems. Contraception is more accessible among the middle class, and abortion is a 'class crime' since the wealthy can always obtain it. De Beauvoir presents what are seen today as familiar arguments for the legalisation of abortion. For example, she argues that it is illegal abortion, not the operation as such, which is the major health risk. De Beauvoir argues that contraception and legal abortion would allow women freedom of choice in maternity: meanwhile women are often obliged to reproduce against their will. In the majority of cases, the mother requires the economic support of a man.

The woman who is pregnant experiences ambivalent feelings; pregnancy is both an 'enrichment' and a 'mutilation': 'The foetus is part of her body and a parasite which exploits it' (*DS* II, p. 307). The pregnant woman is a free human being who has become a passive object. She may comfort herself as to her own value, but this is illusory as she does not really make the baby. Truly creative acts which arise from freedom give objects a necessary value, but the foetus is only a 'gratuitous growth'. The mother does not control the creation of an independent, free being, she only makes it possible. She may compensate by fantasising that her child will be a hero.

At childbirth the woman is again dependent. De Beauvoir argues in favour of medical intervention and the new techniques in childbirth which she believes have reduced mishaps. In contrast to her extensive observations on other aspects of maternity she is reticent on the details of childbirth. The new-born infant creates ambivalence in the mother. The maternal 'instinct' does not exist, and the mother's attitude depends on the total context and her own responses. De Beauvoir does concede that, unless circumstances are extremely unfavourable, the child will be an enrichment for the mother. She finds a satisfaction comparable to that which man looks for in woman – another being who is simultaneously nature and consciousness. The infant is her prey, her double.

Maternal devotion may be lived out in perfect authenticity, but this is rarely so. Usually maternity is a strange mixture of narcissism, altruism, dream, sincerity, bad faith, devotion and cynicism. (*DS* II, pp. 326–7)

This relationship changes as the child grows and the mother may project herself entirely onto the child. 'The great danger which our culture imposes on the child is that the mother to whom it is confided . . . is nearly always dissatisfied' (*DS* II, p. 327). The mother may work out the frustrations of her feelings of inferiority on the child. Some mothers are domineering, if not sadistic. Motherhood does not usually provide the promised self-fulfilment.

The mother-child relationship depends on the sex of the child. Many women prefer sons, on to whom they may project their lost future. Relations with a daughter are more fraught; the mother may seek to make a superior being out of this double or she may wish to impose her own disadvantages upon her. Matters deteriorate when the girl gets older and seeks autonomy. The mother is jealous at first of the daughter's relations with the father. De Beauvoir's vivid account at times betrays her own autobiography, as when she unexpectedly offers the following example: 'often the eldest daughter, the father's favourite, is particularly the victim of her mother's persecutions' (*DS* II, pp. 334–5). According to de Beauvoir, the daughter is seen as a rival for the father's love. Whatever the daughter does, the mother resents her. The mother may become a tyrant to her growing daughter.

De Beauvoir argues against what she considers to be two major prejudices. First is the belief that maternity is sufficient to fulfil a woman's existence. Instead, her relations with her children depend on the total context of her life. Maternity is not a universal panacea. There is nothing 'natural' in undertaking motherhood; it is a moral choice and entails a commitment. Secondly, de Beauvoir challenges the belief that a child is automatically happy with its mother. There are bad mothers, some of whom may inflict real suffering on the infant.

De Beauvoir highlights the contradiction between the contempt held towards women in general and the respect bestowed upon mothers. Paradoxically women are excluded from public affairs and masculine careers only to be charged with the crucial task of forming another human being. Motherhood should include active participation in economic and political life, and child care should be a largely collective undertaking. Then maternity would not be incompatible with outside work. Today, however, they are incompatible partly because work outside the home is often a form of slavery.

The suggestion that mother and child belong exclusively to each other is a 'double oppression'. It is a mystification to assert that maternity brings women equality with men; the single mother is despised. It is only in marriage that the mother is glorified; that is, when she is subordinate to her husband. So long as he remains the economic head of the family, the children will depend on him rather than her. In the home, the housekeeper-mother depends on others for her justification. She cannot assert her own existence and identity.

The first volume of *The Second Sex* sold twenty-two thousand copies in the first week. The publication of the second volume, however, was the most controversial, and 'the critics went wild' (*F Ci*, p. 198). De Beauvoir was accused of being neurotic, frustrated, envious and embittered, and above all she was attacked for her negative view of maternity. Whereas the first volume aims at a more abstract and theoretical argument drawing upon biology, psychoanalysis, history and a critique of male novelists, the second volume is rooted more explicitly in a girl's and woman's daily experience. It is here that the details gain authenticity from the author's concrete observation and experience. This authenticity, which is much more difficult to dismiss than abstract theory, may partly explain the extreme hostility of many male readers and the volume's scandalous success. Mauriac compared it to pornography, which he urged French youth to reject. Camus considered it made the French male look ridiculous. It was attacked by the French right and also put on the Papal black list. (The consequence of this ban continued into the 1960s. In 1962 a copy of the English translation which I sent by post to my sister in Dublin was confiscated by the Irish customs.)

Just as women readers recognised some of their own experience in de Beauvoir's text, so also they responded approvingly to the devastating description of women's general subordination in all spheres. They may not have seen the book as a blueprint for change and liberation, but in it they saw an accurate and original exposition of the overbearing status quo which echoed their own experience. Carole Ascher confesses:

Looking back, I now believe that my own pessimism about women's capacity to choose determined early readings of the book, encouraging me to skip the choice side of the dialectic in favour of the many proofs of oppressive conditions. (1981, p. 130)

De Beauvoir could not see the potential for a specific solidarity of women with separate organisations and the practice of consciousness raising. She could not dream much of liberated alternatives, for there were few such models around her, and no female comrades then jointly to imagine them.

Note

1 See *DS* I, p. 278 or *2nd S*, p. 205; and *DS* 1, p. 292 or *2nd S*, p. 215. When de Beauvoir writes 'The Roman women of decadence, many American women of today, impose their caprices or law upon men' (*DS* 1, p. 302), Parshley excludes the adjective 'American' (*2nd S*, p. 223).

CHAPTER FOUR

RE-READING
The Second Sex

Though de Beauvoir's study now reads differently both for her past and her new readers, the earlier reading cannot be easily jettisoned. The book is part of some women's personal history and part of the history of feminism. This double reading, then and now, is the rationale for my selection of certain themes for a critical discussion.

De Beauvoir's central section on mythology proved startling and evocative to a young woman like myself in the early 1960s. Today, thanks partly to anthropology and to feminists' interrogation of the subject and greater awareness of race and class, it is easier to recognise that de Beauvoir's generalisations fit neither all cultures nor all women. Women readers whose experience in no way approximated that of de Beauvoir were undoubtedly sceptical long ago. From the myths, I have selected for critical discussion those concerned with the female body and sexuality: matters which women now feel freer to talk and write about. De Beauvoir's examination of five male authors stands better the test of time. She initiated a way of looking at 'great' literature from a woman's perspective and there is now a serious body of work in feminist literary criticism. I have also recreated some of my past enthusiasm and mixed response to her text.

In the last decade, a number of women have been concerned to consolidate a theoretical approach to feminism. While the attempt to find the 'origins' or 'first cause' of women's subordination has been largely abandoned, greater emphasis is now placed on explanations for women's continuing subordination and the conditions which could change it. As part of this enterprise, feminists have re-examined Marx and Freud. De Beauvoir's interpretation of these two theorists therefore requires comment. Her extensive debate with biological explanations is of continuing and crucial relevance since the resurgence of sociobiologism in the last decade. The implications of the biological difference between males and females have provoked debates both within feminism and outside it. Considerable space is therefore devoted to various biological explanations and a closer reading of de Beauvoir's text.

My general comments on Volume II of *The Second Sex* invite the reader to place her detailed ethnography of women's lives in a specific context. From this volume, I have selected de Beauvoir's discussion of early childhood which contrasts with her more generalised comments on psychoanalysis and social influences in Volume I. Inevitably the record here of a re-reading has to be selective and cannot do justice to de Beauvoir's enterprise of encyclopaedic proportions (see also Okely, 1984).

In Volume II de Beauvoir does not make use of statistical or in-depth social science studies of women; the latter appeared in strength only from the late 1960s. Instead she draws on the representation of women's experience from psychoanalysts' case studies and literature, especially that written by women. Parshley has tended to retain the evidence from the former and cut the latter. The other major source is personal observation and experience. Insights into the young girl were drawn both from her own past and the many years of teaching in girls' lycées. De Beauvoir sometimes gives examples of friends and acquaintances to back up her argument, making use of the 'continual interest' which she and Sartre had had for many years in 'all sorts of people; my memory provided me with an abundance of material' (*F Ci*, p. 196). Her autobiographies in fact reveal how restricted her acquaintance was with people outside café society and the bourgeoisie.

De Beauvoir has in part done an anthropological village study of specific women, but without the anthropological theory and focus. Her village is largely mid-century Paris and the women studied, including herself, are mainly middle class. There are almost no references to working-class urban women and only rare glimpses of rural, peasant women who still made up the majority of French women at that time. There is just one striking discussion of the burden of the peasant woman in post-war France in the history section (*2nd S*, p. 165). Despite this hidden subjectivity, her observations and her recourse to historical, literary and psychoanalytical documentation raise questions beyond the local study. A paradoxical strength is the hidden use of herself as a case study, and it was one to which many of her women readers intuitively responded. Although in the text she never uses the word 'I' in a personal example, we can, when we examine her autobiography written nearly ten years later, see the link between her own experience and some of her generalised statements about the girl and woman.

● Myths and ideology

The discussion of the myths which surround 'woman' is the core to Volume I. As with her treatment of other aspects, its strength lies in its focused *description* rather than in any convincing *explanation* or first cause of women's subordination. Some later feminists have read the section only for an explanation of women's subordination and thus missed its accumulative impact (see for example Barrett, 1980).

Whether or not she has been misread and simplified, ideas from this section are frequently referred to by feminists and others. De Beauvoir's words hold the imagination by pointing to powerful symbols of 'the feminine' and either explicitly or implicitly challenge their truth. Her description is not neutral, but accompanied by a mocking value judgement. Certain repetitive themes in different ideologies about women are systematically collected together, but de Beauvoir is most convincing in the treatment of western culture. Her description reminds the reader of a long tradition of the 'earth mother' and the 'eternal feminine' which, she argues, while purporting to be laudatory towards woman, is thoroughly dehumanising. The myths which present woman as a powerful symbol mask her effective powerlessness. De Beauvoir's women readers could learn that western myths which were so often said to be complementary to themselves were only mystifications; that is, they served to mask the truth of women's objective subordination and oppression.

The opening pages try to link the myths of the feminine to general existentialist concepts which de Beauvoir has refined by introducing a gender difference. 'Man' needs 'Others' to affirm his existence and to break away from immanence. He engages in projects to achieve transcendence. The female is used by the male as this 'Other' and she remains the object; she never becomes the subject. De Beauvoir does not convincingly explain why woman never becomes the subject, she merely asserts this, yet she described a painful truth of her time.

There are oblique references to Hegel's 'master-slave dialectic', although she does not always bother to name him. She develops Hegel's ideas by contrasting the position of the slave with that of woman. Whereas in Hegel's view the slave is able also to see himself as subject or 'essential' in his struggle with the master, de Beauvoir asserts that woman is in a worse position because she does not see herself as subject and cannot, like the slave, ever see the master (man) as inessential. Whereas the slave can supersede the master, apparently woman cannot supersede man by the same means. In de Beauvoir's view, woman cannot reach the necessary consciousness for emancipation. It is this use of Hegel which later feminist theorists (e.g. Craig, 1979) have teased out of de Beauvoir's text in their analysis of her underlying theoretical position. If woman is deprived even of the potential victory attained by a slave, then it seems that de Beauvoir's message is that woman can never win freedom for herself, except perhaps by some independent change in society and the 'master' male.

If indeed de Beauvoir's Hegelian theory is taken as the major if not sole message of *The Second Sex*, then it would seem that all she is saying is that woman's subordinate state is fixed. But few of de Beauvoir's readers were aware of such embedded theoretical implications. Today it is certainly important to make explicit de Beauvoir's theoretical underpinnings; however, it should not be concluded that these were the key contributions to a past feminist reading of *The Second Sex*.

In contrast to de Beauvoir's preceding examination of biology, psychology, economics and history, the section on myths explores a process whereby women's subordination is continually reaffirmed or 'overdetermined' through ideology. Whether or not de Beauvoir is offering these ideas about women as causes or consequences of women's subordination, she should be credited for pointing to recurrent aspects of the myth of woman, especially in European culture. De Beauvoir sharpened scepticism in her reader.

That woman is the 'Other' is devastatingly stated:

Since women do not present themselves as subject, they have no virile myth in which their prospects are reflected; they have neither religion nor poetry which belongs to themselves in their own right. It is still through the dreams of men that they dream. It is the gods fabricated by males which they adore. (*DS* I, p. 235)

The representation of the world, like the world itself, is the work of men; they describe it from the point of view which is theirs and which they confuse with the absolute truth. (*DS* I, p. 236)

Whereas de Beauvoir's comments on much of European Christian ideology are fairly systematic, her tendency towards generalisations is very misleading when she strays into cultures in another time and space. De Beauvoir selects from social anthropology cross-cultural examples which confirm her argument and avoids reference to the many available counter-examples. To be fair, she does attempt some broad distinctions between Islam, Graeco-Roman culture and Christianity. But otherwise, random cases are plucked from India, Egypt and Oceania, with only occasional counter-examples.

Indeed, the text oscillates between a defiant angry declaration that woman is always 'Other' and a subdued acknowledgement that this view of women may be eclipsed by the presence of some non-female idols in the course of history (*DS* I, p. 234). For example, under dictatorships, woman may no longer be a privileged object, and in the 'authentic democratic society' advocated by Marx, de Beauvoir observes there is no place for 'the Other'. This recognition of broad differences is modified when she notes that Nazi soldiers held to the cult of female virginity and that communist writers like Aragon created a special place for woman. De Beauvoir hopes that the myth of woman will one day be extinguished:

the more that women affirm themselves as human beings, the more the wondrous quality of the Other will die in them. But today it still exists in the heart of *all* men. (*DS* I, p. 235; my emphasis)

This last sentence reveals her continuing need to conclude with a pan-cultural generalisation.

While she is ambivalent as to whether woman as 'Other' is a true universal, she states that 'the Other' is itself ambiguous. It is evil, but 'being necessary for good' it returns to good. Woman embodies 'no fixed concept' (*DS* I, p. 236). In this way, de Beauvoir can explain the apparently conflicting fantasies which women are believed to embody for men. One of these myths is the association of woman with nature. There is a double aspect to this. Nature can be seen as mind, will and transcendence as well as matter, passivity and immanence. On the one hand nature is mind, on the other it is flesh. As evidence for the latter view of nature de Beauvoir looks back to the classical Greek scholars (for example, Aristotle), who asserted that only the male principle is the true creator, while female fertility is merely passive; that is, that woman is the passive earth while man is the seed.

De Beauvoir's examination of classical European writers was helpful to both western and non-western women in exposing the mystification of 'woman' in a long-standing tradition. It was harder for de Beauvoir to look beyond the traditions of her own culture, especially when she had to rely on less accessible sources for a view of nature elsewhere. She offered some examples from India which compare the earth to a mother, but random selections do not prove the universality of any such principle; moreover, her example from Islamic texts where woman is called a field or grapevine (*DS* I, p. 238) is an image from *agriculture* not wild nature. The two are certainly not the same.

Despite these errors, de Beauvoir systematically outlines a dominant European tradition which, since the eighteenth century enlightenment, sees nature as inferior to culture (see Bloch, 1980). Her suggestions about women and nature have stimulated anthropologists to think about the association (see Ardener, 1972). De Beauvoir's link between women and nature is not as absolute as some of her successors have tried to make it (for example, Ortener, 1974). More recently, anthropologists have given examples from other cultures which challenge any pan-cultural generalisation (McCormack and Strathern, 1980). For example Olivia Harris has argued that Indians of the Bolivian Highlands equate the married couple with 'culture' and unmarried persons with 'nature' (1978, 1980); the nature-culture opposition is thus not linked simplistically to a gender opposition.

As elsewhere, de Beauvoir proceeds through the stages of a woman's life. Here, they are examined in the light of external ideology rather than of a woman's concrete experience. Women as a group may comply with and internalise these beliefs as if they were 'natural'. Whereas de Beauvoir tries to suggest that much of the ideology is universal, it was in fact her revelation that this was mere belief, mere myth, which was so powerful to her early readers. Insofar as western women were indoctrinated to believe that they might represent 'mother earth', the 'eternal feminine', erotic temptress or virgin purity, de Beauvoir dismantled these images. Some of us could recognise apparently individual fantasies about ourselves as part of an over-arching tradition made outside us, not born with us; the fantasies were historical, not fixed. The problem for us was how to throw them off. Non-western women, by contrast, gained a novel critical perspective of western ideology which was seen even more as one to reject.

In searching for the basis for certain ideas and myths of woman, de Beauvoir seizes upon woman's capacity to gestate. Her approach is rooted in the European Descartian tradition which separates mind from body. Man apparently would like to be a pure Idea, absolute Spirit, but his fate is to be trapped in the 'chaotic shadows of the maternal belly . . . it is woman who imprisons him in the mud of the earth' (*DS* I, p. 239). De Beauvoir compares the womb to 'quivering jelly which evokes the soft viscosity of carrion' (*DS* I, p. 239). 'Wherever life is in the making – germination, fermentation – it arouses disgust . . . the slimy embryo begins the cycle that is completed in the putrefaction of death' (*2nd S*, p. 178). These extraordinary references to viscosity and slime echo Sartre's extensive discussion of viscous substance both in *Nausea* (1938) and *Being and Nothingness* (1943) and some of his own personal disgust with aspects of the sexual body (see *Adieux*, 1981).

In aiming to deconstruct the myth of the feminine, de Beauvoir thus naïvely reproduces her male partner's and lover's ideas about the female body, while possibly deceiving herself that these are objective and fixed philosophical truths. As in her discussion of biology, she is on dubious ground in suggesting that bodily parts inevitably arouse the same feelings (of disgust) in all individuals and all cultures. She is implying it is 'natural' to look at 'nature' in a specific way. In fact she reveals the extent to which she has internalised both the views of her own culture and the extreme reactions of Sartre.

Her problematic assertions are compounded when she makes unsubstantiated generalisations about primitive people's attitudes to childbirth. In her text such people are an undifferentiated lump and she repeats a clichéd belief that their attitudes to childbirth are always surrounded by the most severe taboos. It is interesting to be informed that childbirth in a number of different societies is subject to elaborate ritual; the danger comes when de Beauvoir implies either that taboos vary according to an evolutionary 'progress' or that attitudes to birth are unvaried. De Beauvoir asserts that all the ancient codes demand purification rites from women in confinement, and that gestation always inspires a 'spontaneous repulsion' (*DS* I, p. 240).

De Beauvoir thus falls into the trap of suggesting that gestation is *naturally* and universally disgusting. Her evidence about so-called primitives is suspect, first because even 'taboos' do not necessarily reflect disgust, and second because a people's cultural treatment of childbirth is linked to differences in descent, marriage and kinship systems and control over offspring. De Beauvoir's assertion that disgust at gestation is spontaneous speaks more of herself and her own time. Today I can criticise de Beauvoir for her suspect generalisation about humanity's spontaneous psychological reactions to the physicality of childbirth, but some twenty years ago I underlined it.

De Beauvoir makes similar sweeping statements about menstruation. She maintains that in all civilisations woman inspires in man the horror of his own carnal 'contingence' – she reminds him of his mortality. This, according to de Beauvoir, is confirmed by an assertion that everywhere before puberty the young girl is without taboo. It is only after her first menstruation that she becomes impure and is then surrounded by taboos. De Beauvoir then offers a random collection of menstrual 'taboos' from Leviticus, Egypt, India, nineteenth-century Britain and France to support this suspect generalisation.

In the 1950s and 1960s this made interesting reading, but it is perilously close to an old-fashioned type of anthropology, exemplified in Frazer's *The Golden Bough*, in which customs are lumped together for their superficial similarity, although in fact they are meaningless when torn from their different contexts. By contrast, a few detailed examples of menstrual taboos in specific cultures are more informative for placing them in context. De Beauvoir does indeed give three such extended examples, but these are excluded by Parshley (*DS* I, pp. 243–6).

In de Beauvoir's view, the taboos associated with menstruation 'express the horror which man feels for feminine fertility' (*DS* I, p. 247). This emphasis on 'horror' is little different from the now discredited view that primitive people's rituals are merely a response to 'fear'. Today, after a wider anthropological reading on these menstrual 'issues' across cultures, I can criticise de Beauvoir's explanation, but I have also to recognise that in 1961 I underlined that single sentence above. Both female writer and reader identified with a myth that woman's body and blood inspired horror and believed it as fact, not fiction. Thus neither de Beauvoir nor the female reader escaped the myths of her own culture.

The myths associated with virginity and the drama of defloration are also discussed by de Beauvoir in terms of psychological fear. Sometimes, de Beauvoir vaguely suggests that customs surrounding defloration have 'mystical' causes, as if this were sufficient explanation. De Beauvoir is at the mercy of outdated European explanations for ritual, partly because any systematic study of rituals associated with women had to await a feminist anthropology.

In recent decades, anthropologists have looked at rituals associated with menstruation, virginity, defloration, pregnancy and childbirth and the connections between a group's specific control over women's sexuality or fertility and the material context. In some societies menstruation will be merely a private event and without ritual taboo. In some cases childbirth and the arrival of a new member to the group will be publicly significant and so

Simone de Beauvoir at work, November 1947

Boulevard St Michel, Paris, 1945

Simone de Beauvoir being addressed by a clergyman, August 1947

LA FEMME MARIÉE

La destinée que la société propose traditionnellement à la femme, c'est le mariage. La plupart des femmes, aujourd'hui encore, sont mariées, l'ont été, se préparent à l'être ou souffrent de ne l'être pas. C'est par rapport au mariage que se définit la célibataire, qu'elle soit frustrée, révoltée ou même indifférente à l'égard de cette institution. C'est donc par l'analyse du mariage qu'il nous faut poursuivre cette étude.

L'évolution économique de la condition féminine est en train de bouleverser l'institution du mariage : il devient une union librement consentie par deux individualités autonomes; les engagements des conjoints sont personnels et réciproques; l'adultère est pour les deux parties une dénonciation du contrat; le divorce peut être obtenu par l'une et l'autre aux mêmes conditions. La femme n'est plus cantonnée dans la fonction reproductrice : celle-ci a perdu en grande partie son caractère de servitude naturelle, elle se présente comme une charge volontairement assumée [1]; et elle est assimilée à un travail producteur puisque, en beaucoup de cas, le temps de repos exigé par une grossesse doit être payé à la mère par l'État ou par l'employeur. En U. R. S. S. le mariage est apparu pendant quelques années comme un contrat inter-individuel reposant sur la seule liberté des époux; il semble qu'il soit aujourd'hui un service que l'État leur impose à tous deux. Il dépend de la structure générale de la société que dans le monde de demain l'une ou l'autre tendance l'emporte : mais en tout cas, la tutelle masculine est en voie de disparition. Cepen-

[1]. Voir vol. Ier.

Page of *The Second Sex* showing Judith Okely's underlinings made in the 1960s

Simone de Beauvoir

Simone de Beauvoir with Jean Paul Sartre and Claude Lanzmann in front of the Great Sphinx at Giza, Egypt 1967

De Beauvoir encounters a Parisian woman beyond her own milieu

imone de Beauvoir on the International Abortion March, Paris, November 1971

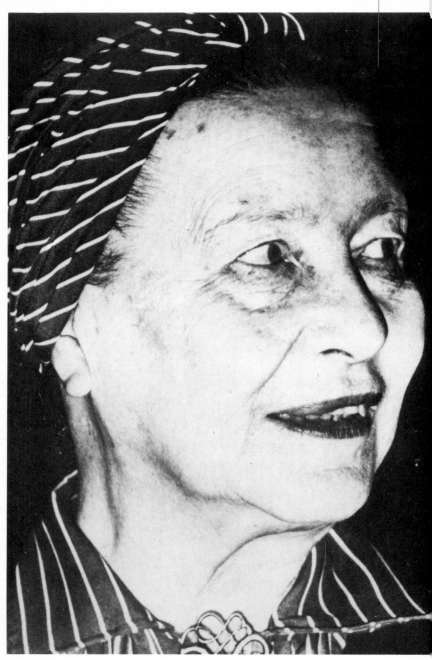

Simone de Beauvoir

marked by ritual elaboration or specific taboos (see La Fontaine, 1972, and Okely, 1983).

De Beauvoir's discussion of the control of women's sexuality and reproduction cross-culturally is in places thoroughly mislead-ing, but in its time it told us about some of the strongest taboos in a specific Judeo-Christian culture, if not class. In 1961 I under-lined in painful recognition her psychological explanation as to the relative importance of virginity:

Depending whether man feels crushed by the forces which encircle him or whether he proudly believes himself capable of annexing them, he either refuses or demands that his wife be handed over as a virgin. (*DS* I, p. 250)

In the 1980s the western bourgeois demand for a virgin wife has all but disintegrated, and *not* because the male has miraculously overcome some innate mystical fear. Changes in attitudes towards female virginity coincide with changes in attitudes to sexuality and marriage and even advances in the technology of birth control. In the early 1960s, as a virgin, I could not see that the bourgeois cult of virginity depended only on the social and historical context. In those days, de Beauvoir's critical discussion of virginity had maximum impact precisely because she mis-takenly argued that it was widely valued in a variety of cultures. Today, we may be more concerned to point to the many counter-examples in order to argue, as she intended, for alternative freedoms. There is a demand for specific case studies rather than broad and inaccurate generalisations.

Inevitably the author's own culture was the most closely observed. It is therefore not surprising that de Beauvoir should suggest that the most disturbing image of woman as 'the Other' is found in Christianity: 'It is in her that are embodied the tempta-tions of the earth, sex and the devil' (*DS* I, p. 270). In the margin I exclaimed 'et on m'a fait Chrétienne!' ('And they made me a Christian woman!'). De Beauvoir, the former Catholic, suggests that all Christian literature intensifies 'the disgust which man can feel for woman' (*DS* I, p. 270), and her examples from modern male writers show the continuing tradition. Again, as elsewhere, she presumed this disgust to be universal and innate. Thus she had not fully freed herself of her own indoctrination into

Christianity when she asserted that its ingredients were general to all societies. But for the reader of the 1950s and early 1960s, de Beauvoir's selection of western traditions, when juxtaposed with a splatter of historical and cross-cultural examples, had a powerful effect. Dominant western beliefs were exposed as of no greater truth than other beliefs and customs.

● Sexism in male literature

In Volume I of *The Second Sex*, de Beauvoir critically examines the collective myth of the 'feminine'[1] in its various forms in the works of novelists, poets or playwrights. De Beauvoir chooses as typical case studies the twentieth-century writers Montherlant, Claudel, Breton and D. H. Lawrence, and one nineteenth-century writer, Stendhal: four French and one English man. She looks at the attitudes towards women expressed by the male characters through the concealed views of the invisible narrator and through the fate of the heroines in the plot. As elsewhere, her analysis hangs on the existentialist notions of 'the Other', bad faith, freedom, transcendence and immanence. Most of the authors treat women as 'the Other', although in varying ways: only Stendhal emerges relatively unscathed by her critique. Today de Beauvoir would be described as having offered an analysis of sexist attitudes in male authors.

The critique of male authors for their mythical representations of women was a relative innovation in literary criticism. Twenty years earlier, Virginia Woolf (in *A Room of One's Own*, 1929) had raised the question of the necessity of economic independence for writing, which women had been largely denied. (De Beauvoir draws upon Woolf in her discussion of the 'independent woman' in Volume II.) Woolf shows how women are indispensable mouthpieces for male writers while in real life they are without power:

Some of the most inspired words, some of the most profound thoughts in literature fall from her lips; in real life she could hardly read, could scarcely spell, and was the property of her husband. (1929, p. 66)

While attacking the sexist privileges of male institutions of education, including Oxbridge, Woolf does not examine sexism in its literary products; unlike de Beauvoir she does not discuss any misrepresentations of women in literature. De Beauvoir has partly inspired and been superseded by a creative explosion of feminist literary criticism. Given her pioneering work, it is therefore somewhat baffling as to why the French publishers, Gallimard, have excluded these chapters from their paperback version.

As elsewhere in *The Second Sex*, de Beauvoir's critique offered a new perspective in familiar places, and is especially significant for women, since the majority of students in literature and the humanities, both in the past and today, are female, while their lecturers and mentors are mainly male. In the late 1950s and early 1960s, the misrepresentation of women in myths (as opposed to an uncritical idealisation) and the problem of women's subordination were rarely discussed in the British or French literary canon. Thus de Beauvoir's attempt to expose men's stereotypes of women penetrated the orthodoxy of even our seemingly gender-free academic studies, not just our personal lives.

A range of feminist studies of literature has since overtaken de Beauvoir.[2] Recently, feminist critics have noted a movement away from 'feminist readings', where the critic focuses on stereotypes of the female or blind spots in the male text, towards the study of women's unique experience and the distinctive aspects of female texts.[3] This is a shift from the feminist reader to the woman writer. Women's writing can be seen as having its own autonomous traditions, although only rarely noticed in the dominant traditions of literary excellence. The new examination of women's writing (sometimes called 'gynocritics') is also concerned with women as language users.[4]

This new approach does not necessarily select and analyse literature by women for its 'greatness' within any conventional hierarchy of literary taste. In some cases the 'trash' novels produced for a mass female readership are examined. Women's writing is studied both for its surface and for its hidden dilemmas. In some cases, the text shows subtle subversions of the prevailing male values and notions of good writing. The woman writer has to work in devious ways to avoid being 'engulfed'.[5] Since the development of literary criticism by feminists, de Beauvoir's comments on male writers' use and abuse of women may have a taken-for-granted look. Even her influence is not always fully acknowledged. Kate Millett's detailed exposé of Lawrence's sexism (1970) gives scant credit to de Beauvoir's earlier study. De Beauvoir's discussion of Montherlant's extreme exploitation of women as sexual objects could also be seen as a precedent for Millett on Henry Miller.

Unlike some of the modern feminist critics, de Beauvoir has little patience for the 'trash' writing of 'lady' authors. In Volume II of *The Second Sex* she also has some dismissive comments for a whole genre of women's writing, namely the confessional, the autobiography and the diary. Some of her observations are indeed pitifully exact; the 'scribblers' and 'dabblers' are pilloried. In rejecting wholesale this genre, she risks repudiating her own practice of autobiographical writing. Moreover, recent feminist writing has particularly stressed the importance of autobiography.

De Beauvoir has been taken to task for belittling even the work of Eliot, Brontë and Austen (Spacks, 1975). She echoes the orthodox criteria for a 'great work' in demanding a panoramic overview of 'big events' such as war, as in Tolstoy, or a 'richness of experience', as in Dostoyevsky, rather than appreciating the microscopic social and psychological detail of domestic and provincial life found in some women novelists. Thus de Beauvoir is herself truly engulfed by the prevailing orthodoxy which later feminists have questioned.

De Beauvoir does make one major use of female literary texts in *The Second Sex*, and that is as documentary sources of women's experience (for example, the work of Eliot, McCullers, Leduc, Colette, Alcott, Parker, Lehmann, Webb, Wharton and Woolf). In practice, she makes extensive use of women's autobiographies and journals as authentic testimony (for example, those of Sophie Tolstoy, Isadora Duncan, Marie Bashkirtseff and Colette Audry). In her use of women's fiction, de Beauvoir has been denigrated for apparently reducing women's literature to social-realist documentation (Spacks, 1975). However, her use is properly selective and in itself imaginative. This use of literary testimony offends social scientists for different reasons – for being merely 'anecdotal', 'descriptive' and 'not generalisable' (see Evans, 1985, p. 73) – when in fact literature can often through one fictional example point to central dilemmas experienced by a mass of individuals. Neither de Beauvoir nor her women readers needed mass empiricist surveys to prove this. There is a certain irony that de Beauvoir is inconsistent in sometimes using male authors' literary descriptions of women as factual sources when it suits her (for example, Balzac, Zola, Hughes, Wright and even her arch critic Mauriac).

Feminist criticism, having explored male texts for 'bias' or limited images of women, then moving on to re-discover female traditions, is now returning to male texts with different interests. The texts are now analysed for what Abel has called 'artful renditions of sexual difference' (1982, p. 2). Gender stereotyping is rarely simple; it has to be created and constantly affirmed. The form it takes will vary just as relations between the sexes change with historical circumstances (see Stubbs, 1979).

Here also de Beauvoir made some preliminary explorations when she linked Montherlant's writing about women and men to his political position and his sympathies with the Nazis during the occupation of France. In her discussion of both Montherlant and Lawrence, de Beauvoir looks at the authors' ideals of masculinity as well as femininity. In some instances it seems that the ideals for their sex presented by the male authors precariously approximates de Beauvoir's own idealisation of men's transcendence. But de Beauvoir ultimately exposes Lawrence's phallocentricism, Montherlant's cult of militarism and his heroes' fear of their own sensuality as absurd masculine ideals. Apart from these passing critical observations, de Beauvoir, as elsewhere, hardly scrutinises the notion of masculinity as an artificial and problematic construction.

The section on the five male authors left its traces twenty years ago. For example, de Beauvoir's critique was understood as a warning to me against the stereotyped and romanticised excesses of Jung, Fromm and hippy California's reinvention of the female archetype in the late sixties. Generally, however, and like many of my contemporaries, I could not sustain a feminist perspective on literature without reinforcement from elsewhere. When reading of inspiring heroes with or without female adjuncts, I identified with the hero as if I were also male. I saw my dissociation from limp heroines as an achievement rather than a betrayal of my sex.

The female reader of the male text may have to do this to avoid defeat. We did not, as readers, then confront our own gender, although almost unknowingly we grasped at any heroines we found worthy of imitation. So despite my absorption of de Beauvoir's critique of Montherlant, when Henry Miller's books were released from their British ban in the 1960s, he succeeded in convincing me that the women whom he so often ridiculed in his writing were lone individuals and did not represent any general view of women. If I wasn't like these 'broads' then it seemed he wasn't insulting women as a whole. I did not see the contradiction when, in the late sixties, a male companion directly identified with Miller, the male author, and his observations of women. He found solace in the text for his own virgin/whore obsession about women. Thus his masculine gender was crucial when reading literature. It took an individual, and a woman, in a stray remark, to clarify for me Miller's habitual but disguised view of all women as mere orifices. The necessary gender blindness of women readers of male texts was only fully confronted as the women's movement spread to literature.

To read only for sexism, as de Beauvoir appears sometimes to do, can of course risk losing everything else. Feminist criticism works alongside other traditions and perspectives. Kate Millett acknowledges that the uncovering of sexism in Lawrence can be made 'without ever needing to imply that he is less than a great and original artist . . .' (1972, p. xii). De Beauvoir's warnings on Lawrence's and Breton's misrepresentations of women did not prevent some of us from celebrating their work. Indeed her warnings were sometimes forgotten in the very areas she had highlighted. Again it was not the academy, but another lone female influence, my friend Margaret, who cooled my euphoria and spelt out in stark terms the fundamental contradiction in Lawrence's demand that women *submit* within an apparently egalitarian partnership in *Women in Love*.

Montherlant is selected by de Beauvoir as a peculiarly nasty example of extreme sexism. For Montherlant, woman represents threatening flesh and is dangerously close to a mother figure. In de Beauvoir's words, Montherlant's woman wallows in immanence. The male author attacks 'the eternal feminine' because in his view it is associated only with specific historical epochs of 'weakness'. But instead of completely dismantling this notion of the eternal feminine, Montherlant, de Beauvoir suggests, merely transforms it – into a monster. 'The ideal woman is perfectly stupid and perfectly submissive' (*DS* I, p. 316). Since women are seen by Montherlant as disgusting sensual flesh, the only physical type he can admire is the muscular woman athlete, but even she is disgusting when she sweats.

De Beauvoir's careful choice of Montherlant from the multitude of male authors recognises that he deserves serious scrutiny; he cannot be written off as idiosyncratic. His ideas, she affirms, belong to a 'long tradition'. Her focus on Montherlant can today be read appreciatively by those feminists who argue that beliefs which degrade and abuse women as objects for humiliation and pleasure are institutionalised and not simply deranged aberrations.

Much of Parshley's translation both of de Beauvoir and the Montherlant quotes is confusing and clumsy. Montherlant's discussion of man's use of women (or horses and bulls) to measure or test his power (*mésurer son pouvoir*) is translated blandly as 'to try one's ability' (*2nd S*, p. 235). Moreover, this significant reference to a *power* relationship is emphasised by de Beauvoir with italics. Parshley has not done so. The recent feminist discussions of power relationships between men and women would not therefore be recognised by English readers in this section as partly anticipated by de Beauvoir.

Parshley also makes significant cuts in de Beauvoir's text. These are not arbitrary, but rooted in sexual politics. Montherlant's hero Costals in *Les Jeunes Filles* (*The Young Girls*) shows a simultaneous disgust and preference for women during their menstruation (*DS* I, p. 237). All this is censored out by Parshley. He omits another passage which de Beauvoir has selected as 'singularly significant': when Costals is considering Solange's need to urinate before coming to bed, he recalls his mare who was so 'proud and delicate' that she never urinated or defecated when he was on her back. De Beauvoir writes:

Here the hatred of flesh is exposed . . . the will to assimilate woman to a domestic animal, the refusal to recognise any autonomy for her, even of the urinary kind; but above all, whereas Costals becomes indignant, he forgets that he also possesses a bladder and colon. (*DS* I, p. 322, and omitted from *2nd S*, p. 238)

This reference to the hero's attitude to a mare/woman neatly contrasts with another example selected by de Beauvoir in her discussion of Lawrence. A male character (Gerald, in *Women in Love*) exerts sadistic control over a mare who is forced to stand foaming in terror near an oncoming train. This instance is used by Lawrence, in contrast to Montherlant, to depict qualities of force which he despises in a hero. The English translation, by omitting the Montherlant example, loses this contrast between authors made by de Beauvoir.

As in much modern literary criticism, she elides the views of the novelist's heroes with details from the author's biography. The heroes are sometimes seen as mouthpieces for the author's beliefs. But sometimes, in contrast to the French text, the English translation omits the passages where de Beauvoir is unambiguously drawing on Montherlant's biography. There are massive omissions from the English version of de Beauvoir's discussion of Montherlant's close relationship with Nazism and his pro-Nazi statements during the German occupation of France. The French edition's thirty-line passage (pp. 324–5) and other references to this subject have disappeared. Thus de Beauvoir's subtle theoretical link between an aesthetic ideology which degrades women and the fascism of a specific historical era is lost.

De Beauvoir selects Lawrence to reveal an alternative approach to women whereby sensuality in the male is celebrated alongside an apparent equality between the sexes. However, in the final analysis, de Beauvoir demonstrates that Lawrence gives superior worth to male sexuality. Woman is ultimately dependent on a superior phallocentric man and sometimes his heroes deny their women orgasms. Man is the initiator through action; woman is positive only on the emotional level. Thus, de Beauvoir argues, Lawrence merely reasserts the traditional bourgeois view.

Claudel's treatment of women is exposed by de Beauvoir as the traditional, Catholic religious view in a new guise. Woman must be self-sacrificing and saint-like. Again, extensive quotes from Claudel are omitted by the translator. Another author, the apparently revolutionary surrealist André Breton, de Beauvoir argues, also idealised and therefore misrepresented woman. In his case, woman is mythologised as peace, magic, the unconscious, nature, the child and eroticism; all in opposition to such things as war and rationality. Again, de Beauvoir concludes, Breton's woman, like so many others, is merely the empty repository for western man's fantasies.

By contrast, de Beauvoir approves of Stendhal because he does not mystify women but portrays them as they are. How reassuring it was to find, through the eyes and maternal guidance of de Beauvoir, a writer like Stendhal who seemed to treat women as people rather than as objects of male fantasy, even though de Beauvoir had to look to the nineteenth century for him. So a prior reading of Stendhal was not unmasked by the female mentor as misguided in the way that the naïve and gender-blind reading of other authors had been. Stendhal's portrayal of women as ultimately dependent on men and therefore flawed could be safely put down to history.

In 1961 I vigorously underlined her observation that Stendhal's woman was 'herself subject' (*DS* I, p. 376). He suggests that women are what their (lack of) education has made them and emphasises the social construction of femininity. Stendhal considers approvingly that women are not mesmerised by the 'sérieux' of the dominant male world view. De Beauvoir claims that in the novel *Lucien Leuwen*, Stendhal is the first (presumably male) novelist to imagine himself authentically into a female character. According to de Beauvoir, Stendhal's heroines act as good existentialists; they choose specific actions, they are authentic. Inauthentic women are denigrated by him. De Beauvoir describes Stendhal's making his heroines overcome struggles. Despite her observation that Stendhal's heroines are not mere functions of the heroes, great emphasis is placed on their liberation through love, and through the love of a man. Here again it seems that de Beauvoir has herself idealised the heterosexual couple as woman's ultimate freedom. Stendhal's women may achieve fulfilment through authentic love, but neither Stendhal nor de Beauvoir in this context imagines alternative authentic futures.

This possibility of 'authentic love' was all very appealing to me, a young virgin, poised for hitherto taboo relationships with men, yet now sceptical about bourgeois marriage. In all optimism I sharply underlined:

If man has only a superficial desire for woman, he will find amusement in seducing her. But it is true love which transfigures his life. (*DS* I, p. 375)

This was what Stendhal explored through the example of Julien Sorel in *Le Rouge et le Noir* (*Scarlet and Black*) and of which de Beauvoir approved. Presumably I, the virgin reader, anticipated transforming someone, instead of being treated as an amusing object of seduction.

Despite de Beauvoir's observations on Montherlant, it seemed to me that his views were those only of an isolated author. I could not yet consider an argument that the treatment of women merely as sexual objects was a general and institutionalised practice which was certainly not symmetrical to any possible treatment that women might attempt to impose on men. Montherlant and his heroes' attitudes were so shocking I could only retaliate in the margins by ingenuously writing that women could also respond in kind towards men, as if this were a satisfactory way out. For some years after, this is what some of us thought we were doing in response to men who treated us as their objects. Only later, as the more explicit discussions in the women's movement progressed, could we recognise that attitudes such as Montherlant's which degrade women might be generalised. The extent of generalisation is, however, a source of controversy. Whereas radical feminism claims, unconvincingly, that male abuse of women is 'elemental' (Dworkin, 1981, p. 68) and unchanging, another feminist perspective rejects any 'essentialist' definition of the male. Instead the degradation of women both in ideology and in practice depends on the specific historical context. Here de Beauvoir's attempt to link Montherlant's views on gender with a fascist regime is illuminating.

The reading of de Beauvoir's critique itself depended on context. The power of representations in literature is hard to dismantle both when it coincides with the dominant order *and* when it appears to break free of it. The sensuality of Lawrence and Breton could be experienced as an intoxicating break from the rigid bodily controls exerted on young women in the 1950s. Breton's surrealist emphasis on chance and coincidence (*le hasard*) was an invitation to adventure in Paris and beyond. Margaret and I retraced Breton's steps as we hitchhiked to Nantes. I embraced Breton's idea of *Mad Love* (*L'Amour Fou*), while only dreamily separating myself from his image of woman which de Beauvoir had exposed as nature, pure poetry and child. Along the 'Boul Mich' I could pretend I was 'Nadja', the distracted Breton heroine with heavily made-up eyes. I imagined myself as mysterious, while inwardly knowing that I was no object.

In anticipation of some meeting with the promised equal partner, I would abandon myself to the imagination and to ethereal encounters. I had fantasies about an earnest young man I never once addressed and who used to stride, eyes upwards, through the Boul Mich, his paralysed left arm stretched behind him. (His handicap, I did not consciously realise, appealed to me because it tempered his masculine power.) We awaited our poets and equal partners, our Sartres who looked like Camus or the actor Gérard Philippe. The latter played Stendhal's Julien Sorel and recited Rimbaud. After *The Second Sex*, I was not going to service this imaginary soul mate, but work as an equal. Like de Beauvoir some of us, her readers, had renounced marriage; like her, some still believed in the heterosexual partnership as an ideal.

Thus de Beauvoir only partially succeeded in challenging the mythology which her women readers might glean from male authors. Although she rejected the institution of marriage, her alternative of the freely chosen partnership was not seen as problematic. She considered that a reasoned choice, ideally between equals, would easily dispose of notions of romantic love. Yet it was the romantic elements in writers like Breton, Lawrence and Stendhal which continued to enchant young women readers and which we confusedly projected back on to de Beauvoir's own partnership with Sartre.

● Biologism

Those who praise de Beauvoir retrospectively invariably quote the opening sentence of Volume II of *The Second Sex*: 'on ne nâit pas femme on le devient':

One is not born, but rather one becomes, a woman; no biological, psychological or economic fate determines the figure that the human female presents in society'. (*2nd S*, p. 295)

The first phrase has been read today by many to mean that woman is socially constructed rather than biologically determined, and de Beauvoir was perhaps most influential precisely because she appeared to challenge biological determinism. However, de Beauvoir's rejection also of economic and psychoanalytic explanations of women's subordination means there is a certain ambiguity here. Her account of the causes gives greater weight to the ideological creation of 'woman' and in turn to women's apparent collusion with or existentialist choice in the matter. Despite de Beauvoir's formal rejection of biological determinism, when the details of her arguments are closely examined it can be seen that she contradicts any claim that biological factors are irrelevant or arbitrary. Again and again she slips into biological reductionism to explain the primary cause of women's subordination.

In the 1980s, with the renaissance of sociobiology and the enthusiasm for biologically determinist causes for social behaviour and subordination, feminist theories are much more alert to latent biologism. De Beauvoir is also now more vulnerable to a current accusation of biologism when subjected to a closer reading.

First let me differentiate the types of biological reductionism. The crudest kind is that which suggests that sexual/physiological differences monolithically dictate the social/psychological and economic differences between male and female. It is useful to distinguish sex and gender; sex is a purely physiological/genetic/biological fact; gender is the social construction, the range of variable characteristics attributed to and acquired by males and females. The physiological differences in this definition are not considered to have a direct and single causal consequence for gender, because the notions of male and female *gender* distinctions vary across time and place, historically, cross-culturally and also within the same society, depending on class and ethnic identity. The crudest biological-determinist argument claims that the physiological differences in reproductive organs and in fat distribution between the sexes, and the fact that only women gestate, lactate and menstruate, automatically account for the different work done by men and women (the sexual division of labour). The physiological differences are said to explain the subordination of women or the so-called complementarity of roles. Strangely, some Marxist feminists have recently fallen into the trap of suggesting that women's singular biology should be considered as the 'material base' to gender divisions (Brenner and Ramas, 1984). This is a travesty of the Marxist concept of materialism and has been adequately rejected by Barrett (1984).

Sociobiologists have introduced a more flexible interpretation of biological determinism; namely, that over millennia of evolution, this sexual difference has brought a necessary and highly programmed adaptation in behaviour. Thus each sex is said to be genetically programmed towards certain types of behaviour. Aggression is associated with males while emotional nurturing is associated with females. Given the millennia of programming, this is not changeable. However, sociobiologists have invariably taken very specific western notions of gender and presumed that all societies are of an 'individualistic', competitive type, as found under capitalism and where sociobiologists consider that competitive aggression is the 'civilising' factor. They then look for such characteristics in animals and ignore anything which does not fit their western stereotypes. Unlike the sociobiologists, de Beauvoir's tendency towards biological reductionism does not extend to the suggestion that each sex is genetically programmed to behave in specific, rigid ways. However, there are times when she over-elaborates the consequences of the female's capacity to gestate and lactate, using it to explain an inevitable division of labour between men and women.

Another more sophisticated form of biological reductionism is the assertion that *perceived* sexual/bodily differences between males and females will inevitably cause the same ideas and social reactions – that the physical differences inevitably stimulate all societies to make the *same* value judgement, so that one sex, the female, is seen as inferior to another. Thus there is the now-hackneyed argument that because the male genitals protrude this explains why they are valued, and because a woman's genitals do not protrude in the same way this explains why they are undervalued. We should make a clear distinction between the penis the physical object and the phallus, the psychic symbol of the penis. It cannot be presumed in all societies for all time that the penis should be seen as the powerful phallus. There is no inevitable reason why a protrusion should be valued and a cavity not. Indeed even in western Europe powerful symbolic value is attached to dark holes. There is no *inevitable* explanation as to why a hard object – the ideal state for the penis in heterosexual intercourse – should be valued over a soft, wet object, the ideal sexual state for the vagina. These value judgements are deeply embedded in so-called neutral subjects: for example, in academia 'hard' subjects like science are valued over 'soft' data and 'soft' subjects like literature. Despite her declared position, de Beauvoir slides into a secondary biological explanation for women's subordination and the sexual division of labour. Insofar as women's subordination is explained by a fixed, unchanging *ideological interpretation* of sexual, physical difference, then it would appear that nothing can ever be changed except through surgery, chemistry and the laboratory. De Beauvoir does not take such a line, but there are double messages in her text.

First, de Beauvoir argues that women's subordination is *constructed* both from the outside by the dominant set of beliefs and from the individual's collusion, if she, the woman, fails to choose otherwise. This subordination of women is, according to her celebrated quote, not determined by any biological, psychological or economic 'destiny'. The sentence 'one is not born but rather becomes a woman' cannot be considered as a materialist explanation, which emphasises external conditions.

De Beauvoir argues for the construction, albeit only ideological rather than materialist, of the category woman. There is, on the other hand, a second half-hidden and contradictory message which is as follows: De Beauvoir alleges that women's physiology, her body and her allegedly 'special' kind of eroticism explain why she is always identified as the Other, as the object rather than the subject; why, while man can find 'transcendence' in their bodies and sexuality, women are fated to 'immanence'. De Beauvoir suggests that men find autonomy through their bodies but women are less likely to do so: woman is the victim of the species, is enslaved to it. While men in their brief reproductive role can retain their individuality, women come into conflict with the long-term interest of the species. Whereas animals merely repeat and maintain the species, man (not mankind) creates and invents in accord with the transcendent possibilities open to human beings. In contrast to men, women's reproductive role obliges women only to maintain rather than create. Here we see not only a biological reductionism in de Beauvoir, but also a rejection of the creative significance of social reproduction, the upbringing of children – something for which both males and females could be equally responsible.

Today, feminists may gasp at this biologism. It seems like a permanent trap from which we, women or men, cannot escape. We cannot easily change our bodies. However, some radical feminists have, without even de Beauvoir's ambiguity, confused sex with gender and advocated a solution which is consistent with such biologism. Shulamith Firestone, for example, proposes the substitution of test-tube fertilisation and mechanical wombs in laboratories to rid women of biological reproduction (1972). This does not resolve the more crucial long-term problem of the upbringing and care of children, nor does it confront the fact that in a patriarchal society men direct and control the laboratories which in turn are governed by the state.

De Beauvoir's readers in the 1950s and 1960s, and here I use experience as part guide (see also Ascher, 1981), reacted favourably to de Beauvoir's account of maternity. They responded to the raw and negative description of the physiological, near animal, burden of maternity which defied the prevailing sentimental view of the maternal instinct, its naturalness and its supposedly unadulterated pleasure. Even though de Beauvoir sometimes falls into the kind of biological reductionism which elsewhere she was trying to attack, the important difference between her description of maternity and that of post-war propaganda lies in the evaluation. De Beauvoir described maternity with disgust, as something degrading and in conflict with the existentialist ideal of individual self-development. It came to us as a revelation that the foetus and infant could be depicted as a parasite of our bodies. Some of us gladly embraced these images of a growing monster in the belly, threatening our identity rather than extending it. We wanted the language to reject maternity and motherhood which then seemed to demand that women retreat to the marital home and nuclear family.

Let us examine in detail some of the evidence of de Beauvoir's inadvertent secondary biologism in Chapter I of Volume I entitled 'The Biological Facts'. Despite her claims that biology is no explanation for women's subordination, de Beauvoir attributes fixed values and inflexible consequences to the biological differences between males and females. Whereas she argues that no symbolic significance can be read into the differences between egg and sperm and conception by ejaculation and implantation into the womb, she nevertheless introduces a value-loaded hierarchy or asymmetry to the act of sexual intercourse, male animal decoration, the genitalia, menstruation, birth, lactation and the menopause. She also collapses the description of non-human mammals into that of humans.

A close reading reveals that de Beauvoir implicitly suggests that either the anatomical differences between males and females inevitably induce ideas of subordination or that biological differences are inevitably debilitating for women. Although she distinguishes the phallus from the penis, and already in the 1940s has read and used the French psychoanalyst Lacan, who clarified this distinction and has influenced some later feminists (for example, Mitchell, 1974), de Beauvoir still claims that the penis *naturally* provides a 'tool' for transcendent identity.

Early on in the chapter, de Beauvoir asserts that there is no necessity for the body to have a particular structure: 'it is possible to imagine a society which reproduces itself by parthogenesis (without sexual union) or one composed of hermaphrodites' (*DS* I, p. 40). When discussing the part of chromosomes, she denies the passivity of the female since both the male and female play an equal part. She ridicules some people's suggestion that since gestation takes place in a stable organism, the womb, women likewise should remain in another stable place, the home! (*ibid.*, p. 47). Fine stuff. De Beauvoir is here arguing against any secondary biologism, but she loses her head when she moves on to vertebrates:

The female organism is wholly adapted for and subservient to maternity, while sexual initiative is the prerogative of the male. The female is the victim of the species . . . during certain periods in the year . . . her whole life is under the regulation of the sexual cycle. (*2nd S*, p. 52)

We are gently led by de Beauvoir to apply observations about non-humans to humans. In sexual intercourse:

It is in birds and mammals especially that he (the male) forces himself upon her . . . Even when she is willing or provocative, *it is unquestionably the male who takes the female*. She is taken. In this penetration her inwardness is violated, she is like an enclosure that is broken into. (*2nd S*, p. 53; my emphasis)

Parshley's use of the concrete image of an enclosure emphasises the physical dimension, missing the person's state of mind. By contrast, my translation of the last sentence emphasises the psychoanalytical resonance in de Beauvoir: 'She appears like an interior state which is violated' (*DS* I, p. 57). De Beauvoir gives an extremely subjective view of the mechanics of sexual intercourse. According to her, a man's 'domination is expressed in the very posture of copulation'. The man's organ is 'a tool', whereas the female organ is 'only an inert receptacle' (*DS* I, p. 57). Here de Beauvoir is imposing a value-loaded interpretation on to the biological facts. Yet earlier, she condemns others for a value-loaded interpretation and dismisses some people's assertions about anatomy as just mediaeval symbolism (*2nd S*, p. 46). To describe the vagina as merely an inert receptacle is also to be guilty of limited symbolism.

Moreover, she is guilty of anthropomorphism in introducing experiences of violation and 'interiorities' when commenting on non-human mammals. She makes no distinction between a human who reflects on his or her experience of sexual intercourse and an animal which does not. De Beauvoir states that among almost all animals the male is 'on' the female. She has to find maximum significance in the metaphor. Yet she has not even got her facts correct for non-human primates, since female monkeys do not lie on their backs. Moreover, the latters' half-squatting position, baring their buttocks in intercourse, could in fact be interpreted as aggressive not passive if adopted by humans. Perhaps de Beauvoir is thinking of the missionary pose which has sometimes been argued by western middle-class men as evidence of male domination, but the speakers merely expose their own gymnastic rigidity and cultural bias. (I recall being given this argument by a Parisian male in 1961, and was too sexually naive to refute him.)

The process of fertilisation is also value loaded by de Beauvoir: 'The fundamental difference between the male and female' is that the male in ejaculating his sperm 'recovers his individuality'; it separates from the body while a fertilised egg remains in the female. 'First violated, the female is then alienated . . . she becomes in part another than herself' (*2nd S*, p. 54). It could as well be argued that a man is alienated because he is never sure that he has successfully reproduced. De Beauvoir also lights up on the 'magnificent and gratuitous' plumage of the male as a sign of power and individuality. This again is a partial reading both of animals and humans. First, not all male animals are beplumed. Secondly, today, popularist sociobiologists explain western women's decorative fashions as the result of biological programming. These explanations are inconsistent. Bright 'plumage' among women can be interpreted instead as a sign of decorative dependence.

De Beauvoir describes the strong independence of the male animal whose 'urge towards autonomy . . . is crowned with success . . . he leads a more independent life and his activities are more spontaneous . . . it is always he who commands' (*2nd S*, p. 56). First, the non-human male's 'command' is questionable, it depends on interpretation. Secondly, de Beauvoir reveals an existentialist value judgement which privileges autonomy and independence. Later feminists have stressed the values of co-operation and group solidarity for survival and argue that these values may in turn give a greater sense of fulfilment to the individual. Feminist historians and anthropologists have explored the solidarity of groups of women in the past and present, while the consciousness-raising groups and collectives of the women's liberation movement have worked to create and reinforce solidarity.

Puberty for the girl is seen by de Beauvoir as a crisis because of physiological changes such as menstruation. She neglects to discuss puberty in males, when genital and hair growth and voice change might also be interpreted as a crisis. Her interpretation is arbitrary. 'It is during her periods that she feels her body most painfully as an obscure, alien thing . . . Woman, like man, *is* her body, but her body is something other than herself' (*2nd S*, p. 61). She presumes that all women see menstruation as some confirmation of a separation between the self and the body. Yet equally the male seminal flow, especially in wet dreams, could be seen as self/body separation. De Beauvoir's view is governed by the Judeo-Christian perception of menstruation as polluting and threatening. Her focus on the possible pain of menstruation for some individual women can indeed be accepted as a biological fact. The implications, however, are also controversial, and the way society deals with this fact will vary historically (see Sayers, 1982, pp. 110–24).

A similar emphasis on the pain and physiological risks of pregnancy is made by de Beauvoir. 'Woman experiences a more profound alienation when fertilisation has occurred' (*2nd S*, p. 62). She points critically to the post-war cult of maternity: 'contrary to an optimistic theory whose social utility is all too obvious . . . gestation is fatiguing work which does not offer individual benefit to the woman and on the contrary demands heavy sacrifices' (*DS* I, p. 66). The pregnant woman's frequent vomitings are seen by de Beauvoir as an indication of the organism's rebellion against the species which is gradually taking possession of the woman. In a footnote, de Beauvoir acknowledges that she is describing maternity solely from the physiological point of view and adds that 'maternity can be very rewarding psychologically for a woman, just as it can also be a disaster' (*DS* I, p. 66). Thus any deference to the joys of maternity is immediately negated by the punchline. These passages are heavily underlined in my 1961 copy of *Le Deuxième Sexe*. Yet today these same passages provoke anger among a younger generation of feminists.

De Beauvoir declares that there is an incompatibility between the demands of the individual and those of the species. Breastfeeding is described primarily by her as tiring and detrimental to the mother. Women have a hostile element embedded in them; 'it is the species which gnaws at them' (*DS* I, 67). There is no discussion of any sensual pleasure, nor of the contraction of the womb during breastfeeding. The focus is on the woman as victim.

Although biological determinists of the right have also used the facts of childbearing and lactation to justify women's dependency and subordination, the same facts have been presented rather differently by de Beauvoir. I suggest that only a woman would describe the foetus and infant as a threat to the female adult. No man has to consider pregnancy as a possible experience for himself, although he might think of the *social* responsibility of fatherhood as a threat to his autonomy. To this extent, the different physiologies of male and female have different implications for each sex, but there is no *necessary* reason why a female should see maternity as a threat to her individuality: she could as well feel more complete.

Women's reproductive capacity and experience are continually seen by de Beauvoir as an enslavement. The woman's loss of fertility at menopause, albeit another crisis, is represented as a liberation. De Beauvoir also suggests there are greater instabilities in women, giving a biological or hormonal explanation for their 'hysterical' behaviour (*2nd S*, p. 64). Yet women's hysteria could be seen as the rational disruptive response of the repressed who refuse to accept the dominant language of their 'reasoned' oppressors. Recently feminists have begun to explore how men's apparently lesser ability to cry is linked with the social cult of masculinity.

Throughout this chapter on the biological facts, de Beauvoir slips from an apparently neutral description of the differences between male and female to one which idealises the so-called male qualities. Not only is the male presented as larger and more 'robust' but he is also more 'adventurous' and 'independent', with more 'spontaneous activities'. He is described approvingly as more 'conquering' and more 'imperious' (*DS* I, p. 60). The male's genital life does not conflict with his personal existence; it apparently unfolds in a continuous way, 'without crisis and generally without accident' (*DS* I, p. 69). De Beauvoir does not consider the many instances when males do not and cannot live up to her biological ideal, when they *fail* to command or when impotence prevents penetration and reproduction. De Beauvoir's refusal to consider male sexuality and masculinity as problematic occurs throughout her work.

De Beauvoir asserts that among all female mammals 'in no

other is enslavement of the organism to the reproductive function more imperious nor more difficult to accept' (*DS* I, p. 69). This I also once underlined. There seemed no inconsistency to me then between such biological reductionism and my underlined approval of de Beauvoir's concluding argument in this opening chapter. Since my own reproductive function seemed so difficult to accept, it seemed 'natural' that this could be universal. Some recent feminist discussion also finds no inconsistency and applauds de Beauvoir for her consideration of both biology and its social interpretation (Sayers, 1982). Yet de Beauvoir's conclusions belie many of the biologically fixed explanations of her detailed discussion. While considering that the biological facts are one of the keys to understanding women, she denies that women have a fixed destiny: 'They are not enough to define a hierarchy of the sexes; they do not explain why woman is the Other; they do not condemn her to remain in this subordinate role for ever' (*DS* I, p. 70). De Beauvoir also states that the significance of physical strength depends on the varying social context. In passing comments she suggests that the female regains in maternity another type of autonomy, and that in many cases, even among animals, the male's co-operation is necessary in the care of the young. Finally, she asserts that a society's customs cannot be deduced from biology. Thus, in her general overview she reasserts the importance and variability in the interpretation by human beings of the physiological facts. As it happens, her own interpretation of those facts does not break free of her personal and historical context.

● Psychology and psychoanalysis

In the second type of explanation, de Beauvoir attempts to examine an alternative explanation: from psychology or, in effect, psychoanalysis. Her critique of Freud is, according to Mitchell (1974), founded on a misreading and misinterpretation of his work, with which she seems to have only a scant acquaintance. Freud is presented by de Beauvoir as saying simplistically that women are doomed to inferiority because of their 'penis envy'. De Beauvoir attributes a biological reductionist interpretation to Freud's celebrated statement 'anatomy is destiny', which could instead be read as a description of society's treatment of the two sexes. Certainly some later psychoanalysts, the post Freudians, are often guilty of a biological reductionist interpretation, but Mitchell has attempted to argue that Freud was merely describing the position of women in his epoch, in middle-class Vienna, rather than asserting any fixed generalisation. De Beauvoir's distinction between the biological penis and the ideological phallus as well as her emphasis on the different social significance attributed to the two sexes in infancy (Volume II of *The Second Sex*) are, according to Mitchell, consistent with Freud's 'real view'.

Ironically, de Beauvoir sets up her Freudian straw man and attacks him with arguments which contradict aspects of her own preceding chapter on biology. In the chapter on psychoanalysis, there is no ambiguity in her critique of biological reductionism. Mitchell suggests that de Beauvoir's misrepresentation of Freud is responsible for a string of misreadings by later feminists (for example, Firestone 1970), who seem not to have read much Freud at source. Not surprisingly, psychoanalysis was for a while caricatured and reviled by members of the women's movement. Yet de Beauvoir made extensive use of psychoanalysis elsewhere in *The Second Sex*, including case studies from analysts as scientific evidence in Volume II.

More recently, feminists have begun to reinterpret and elaborate ideas from psychoanalysis, looking at the construction of gender within early family relations (for example, Chodorow, 1978). Possible sexism in the works of Freud and the French psychoanalyst and theorist Lacan have been confronted. There is disagreement as to whether the power of the phallus is universal and a-historical (see Mitchell, 1974, and Wilson, 1980). Infantile sexuality and the concept of the unconscious are recognised as significant determinants and are not necessarily seen as inconsistent with a Marxist-feminist interpretation of women's subordination.

But whether or not de Beauvoir misread Freud, she has consistently denied the existence of infantile eroticism, the lasting effects of childhood relationships and the concept of the unconscious. The latter would contradict her existentialist philosophy which denies the intrusion of any such determining factor on an individual's reasoned ability to choose and change in the spontaneity of the moment. Despite de Beauvoir's theoretical position, I argue that aspects of her fiction and autobiography in fact demonstrate the continuing power of unconscious forces which surface now and then to challenge her rational control (see Chapters 2 and 5).

● Engels and economism

Having formally rejected biological and psychological explanations for the subordination of women, de Beauvoir attempts to examine an economic one. Her main text is Engels' *The Origin of the Family, Private Property and the State* (1884), without a wider analysis of materialist/Marxist explanations. She concludes that an 'economic' explanation is unsatisfactory and returns to one drawn from existentialism, although with some commitment towards socialism. In 1961 I responded favourably to de Beauvoir's stray remarks like 'the fate of woman and that of socialism are intimately linked' (*DS* I, p. 98). It is now recognised by de Beauvoir, her admirers and her critics, that such a remark demands something more specific both in theory and practice.

As in the case of her discussion of psychoanalysis, de Beauvoir has a favourable comment for aspects of a Marxist, historical materialism because it recognises humanity not as an animal species but as an historical and changing reality. Human society does not submit passively to nature but rather takes control of it, not through anything subjective and internal, but through 'praxis' (a Marxist term translated by Parshley as 'practical action', *2nd S*, p. 84). 'The consciousness which woman makes of herself . . . reflects a situation which depends on the economic organisation of society' (*DS*, I, p. 96). Thus de Beauvoir acknowledges a link between beliefs or ideology and the economic 'mode of production' in a standard Marxist sense. The latter term, whose definition continues to be debated, is used broadly to describe the different forms of organisation, control and distribution of a society's economic resources. Two examples of different modes of production are the feudal and capitalist systems. De Beauvoir then proceeds to reject what is now regarded by many Marxist theorists as a crude 'economism', namely the assertion that everything can be crudely and directly reduced to an economic cause without intervening factors. Sometimes, when she thinks she is making a critique of Engels, she is in effect attacking classical *non*-Marxist economics; that is, she rejects a view 'that perceives in man and woman no more than economic units' (*2nd S*, p. 91). A Marxist would surely also agree. She misunderstands both Engels' and others' view of a wider materialist explanation. The notion of the profit-calculating 'economic man' which she attacks really belongs to classical bourgeois economics.

Engels looks at the divisions of the sexes in early history. De Beauvoir appears in this section to accept uncritically Engels' belief, which has since been discredited by most feminist anthropologists, that in earlier hunting and gathering societies there was equality, although a division of tasks between the sexes. She considers that women did productive work like pottery and weaving, but wrongly assumes that they remained at the 'hearth' (*DS* I, p. 96) while men were out hunting and fishing. De Beauvoir had to depend at that time on the heavily male-biased view of early history. Feminist anthropologists have since obliged the 'experts' to recognise the crucial role of women as gatherers and foragers in hunting *and* gathering societies. Women could hardly accomplish this at the hearth, and indeed ranged many miles from the camp. Moreover, gathering often provided the vital staple food while the meat from hunting could be only an occasional luxury.

Engels explains women's subordination by the advent of private property, which he considers came with animal breeding and agriculture. Women then became property and men demanded monogamy to ensure legitimate heirs. De Beauvoir accepts Engels' description of the changes, but is not convinced by his explanation. The concept of individual ownership, she says, must be preceded by a concept of individual autonomy. This would, however, remain subjective without the practical means to satisfy it in the external world. She then paints a stereotyped western view of primitive society in which people are allegedly a helpless prey to 'superstitious' beliefs. All is changed, she considers, with the material invention of the bronze or iron tool, but even this is insufficient, for it depends on the *attitude* of the man wielding it: 'an attitude that implies an ontological infrastructure' (*DS* I,

p. 100). Her emphasis on 'the tool' reflects the bias of the early historians who saw the 'phallic tool' as the only mark of culture. She does not consider how or indeed whether the male monopolised the bronze tool. De Beauvoir then offers what she later admits to be an 'idealist' explanation for male dominance; that is, she considers the primary causal factor to be people's ideas rather than any conditions which affect those ideas. In this case, the major explanation lies in man's, not woman's, wish to treat the opposite sex as 'Other'. Enslavement of any kind results from:

the imperialism of the human consciousness seeking always to exercise its sovereignty objectively. If the human consciousness had not included the original category of the Other and an original aspiration to dominate the Other, the invention of the bronze tool could not have caused the oppression of women. (*2nd S*, p. 89)

Thus she explains male domination unconvincingly as a result of the male's allegedly inherent wish to dominate.

In recent years, a more sophisticated materialist/Marxist approach to the study of gender, as well as of class and race, would also reject the crude economism attacked by de Beauvoir. At the time, she showed minimum evidence of having read Marx and thus her comprehension of materialism was limited. Throughout *The Second Sex*, any attempt to link gender with a class analysis is missing. Years later de Beauvoir confessed that if she were now faced with writing *The Second Sex* her approach would differ:

I should provide a materialistic, not an idealistic, theoretical foundation for the opposition between the Same and the Other. I should base the rejection and oppression of the Other not on antagonistic awareness but upon the economic explanation of scarcity . . . this would not modify the argument . . . that all male ideologies are directed at justifying the oppression of women, and that women are so conditioned by society that they consent to this oppression. (*ASD*, pp. 483–4)

However, when de Beauvoir later inserted materialism into a study of another category, the aged (1970), the results are unconvincing (see Evans, 1985, p. 112).

Some feminist theorists, while continuing to reject Engels' hopelessly inadequate armchair anthropology and the assumption that many pre-capitalist societies were marked by equality between the sexes, have nonetheless been stimulated by his attempt to link changes in the subordination of women to changes in the larger economy or mode of production (see Sacks, 1974, and Delmar, 1976). In this sense de Beauvoir's idealist critique of Engels and of materialist explanations has subsequently been rejected.

● The experience of womanhood

In Volume II of *The Second Sex*, de Beauvoir attempts to describe through the various stages of a woman's life how she is *made* feminine. It is at the opening of this volume, entitled 'L'Expéri-ence Vécue' or 'Lived Experience' (translated by Parshley as 'Woman's Life Today'), that we find the celebrated statement, already partially quoted:

> One is not born, but rather becomes a woman. No biological, psychic, or economic destiny determines the figure that the human female assumes in the midst of society; it is civilisation as a whole that elaborates this creature, intermediary between male and eunuch, which is classified as feminine. Only the intervention of others can establish an individual as an *Other*. (*DS* II, p 13)

The last sentence confirms her existentialist explanation that woman is seen as Other; however, de Beauvoir is not very convincing as to *why* this should occur.

Volume II places its arguments in a detailed description of the girl's and woman's actual experience rather than in ideological representations of 'woman'. De Beauvoir gives the impression that this is a description of the experience of *all* women at *all* times. This suggestion is highly suspect, especially in the light of today's more detailed and solid research, although there are still feminist theorists who take their white, western and ethnocentric model as universal, with scant regard for other cultures and the specificity of race (Carby, 1982). De Beauvoir somewhat defeats her case that woman is made, not born, by resorting to a universalistic language as if 'woman' or 'the young girl' always apparently experienced life as de Beauvoir described it. To be fair, the single-paragraph Introduction to Volume II states:

When I use the words 'woman' or 'feminine' I obviously refer to no archetype, no changeless essence whatever; the reader must understand the phrase, 'in the present state of education and custom' after most of my statements. (*2nd S*, p. 31)

However, this warning still ignores class and race and is quickly forgotten, especially in the translation, where Parshley moves it to the opening of Volume I. Sometimes her generalised descriptions conceal not only a cultural, class and historical bias but also a very personal experience – that of herself. This becomes clearer when passages in her *Memoirs* are found to echo descriptions of the young girl in *The Second Sex*. To this extent, de Beauvoir's analysis draws on concrete evidence which has sometimes been overlooked. For example, in a recent study, Mary Evans rightly finds severe limitations in *The Second Sex* insofar as it lacks a material base:

Materialists among feminists have been on much firmer ground in their accounts of sexual relations . . . different wage rates . . . Discrepancies in . . . access to social and political power can all be demonstrated from 'evidence drawn from social reality'. (1985, p. 73)

Evans does not, however, notice the concealed ethnography in de Beauvoir, who uses literature and documentary case studies only as illustrations of a pre-existing and coherent account of her own circle and some others. Thus de Beauvoir's text is lacking neither specific evidence nor first-hand field work from 'social reality'; the severity of its limitations lies in what she chooses to observe and to omit. Given that she relies so much on personal experience, she does not or cannot escape her class and cultural entourage, and all the while she remains blissfully unaware of such limits. Part of this is explained by her belief in individual free choice which existentialism emphasises over all wider determinants. De Beauvoir thus feels free to ignore the class and cultural specificity of her relatively privileged circle.

Instead of rejecting de Beauvoir wholesale because she is proved to be merely 'subjective', I argue that it is the very specificity of her material which, in its time, gave the book its appeal, both to those who shared some of her experience and those who did not. Her generalisations, especially in Volume II, are grounded in concrete experience, however limited. The vivid detail aroused public hostility and yet privately inspired many white, middle-class women who recognised some parallel experience embedded in her text. It could be read by women of another race and culture as an internal critique of the west, and some of them also found parallels in their own gender or class position. And testimonies of the Middle Eastern and Indian women (see Chapter 1) record their appreciation of de Beauvoir's mere act of questioning.

Volume II has three major sections. First, 'Formation', which deals with the different stages of the female from infancy to puberty and sexual initiation. De Beauvoir's account of early infancy develops some of the biological and psychoanalytical points raised in Volume I, but while more emphasis is placed here on the social and experiential factors which go to create the gender of the child, there are again traces of biological reductionism, despite de Beauvoir's avowed rejection of this.

De Beauvoir offers an explanation for the different gender identities: 'only the intervention of others can establish an individual as an *"Other"*' (*DS* II, p. 13). She suggests that the child alone would not be able to imagine herself or himself as sexually differentiated. If people notice that a girl even from infancy is sexually specified, this is not because

mysterious instincts directly doom her to passivity, coquetry, maternity; it is because the influence of others upon the child is a factor almost from the start, and thus she is indoctrinated with her vocation from her earliest years. (*2nd S*, p. 296)

She does not support any suggestion that gender identity is significant at a pre-verbal stage.

At some point after weaning, boys are expected to be more independent of the mother than girls. In this sense girls are privileged. The boy is persuaded by the mother or nurse that more is demanded of him because he is superior. This is confirmed through a concrete object: his possession of the penis. To this extent de Beauvoir's argument is that the power given to the penis as phallus is a social not a biological fact. However, now and again she verges on a 'natural' explanation. 'Anatomically, the penis is well suited for this role, detached from the body' (*DS* II, p 18). De Beauvoir says it seems like a 'natural little plaything, a sort of doll' (Parshley misleadingly translated doll/*poupée* as puppet, *2nd S*, p. 299).

Generally de Beauvoir's explicit argument is that a child's different anatomy does not *inevitably* produce a sense of superiority or inferiority. Those feelings are stimulated by the way in which adults encourage the child to think about his or her anatomy: mothers and nurses encourage a boy's pride in his penis, but do not draw attention to the girl's genitals. De Beauvoir rejects both a psychoanalytical theory (be it Freudian or not) of a girl's inevitable penis envy and a castration theory; it depends whether she is already dissatisfied with her situation.

De Beauvoir's ambivalence between social or biological causes is made more explicit when she suggests that the penis, as an external object which can be taken hold of, is a useful means for the boy to project the mystery of his body on to something outside himself. The penis can, she says, be a symbol of autonomy, transcendence and power. Although a little boy might fear castration, de Beauvoir suggests that this is easier to overcome than the vague fear which the little girl has towards her 'insides', a fear 'which often will be perpetuated throughout her life as a woman' (*DS* II, p. 25). De Beauvoir gives a gender twist to the existentialist idea that a person becomes free by projecting herself or himself into transcendent activities by suggesting that only the male can 'naturally' find this transcendence through the body. Again, therefore, we find the hint of anatomical determinism. Apparently the woman's genitals are doomed to be seen only as 'an envelope which is not to be grasped by hand, in a sense she has no sex' (*DS* II, p. 18).

De Beauvoir does not explore the possibility that the female genitals are more than mere absences. The western, Judeo-Christian tradition has encouraged the perception of female genitals as a blank space, when in fact the mons venus with pubic hair, the labia major and minor, clitoris and entrances could be considered highly visible. They are indeed *made* invisible in much of European sculpture and painting. The female genitals can in fact be viewed as a voracious mouth rather than as a mere gap. Many western women have been *made* to treat them as invisible.

The absence of ink marks in the early pages of my 1961 copy

of Volume II confirms de Beauvoir's statements about the repression of female sexuality; it reflects not only the age, gender, culture and class of the reader but also the epoch. The first recorded contact between author and virgin reader appears when illuminating social statements are made about the construction of sexual shame and gender asymmetry. If de Beauvoir's anatomical discussions elicited anything, it had to be repressed. Today, I can freely and casually take her to task for treating the female genitalia as a blank. In the past, if not today, the male genitals were for many young women also made mysteriously blank; that is, on a conscious level. We were not to know about such things until the wedding night. De Beauvoir's 'forward' discussion of the penis and of little boys urinating seemed vaguely disgusting and certainly threatening to a female product of a single-sex upbringing.

This is not to say that the male genitals and their phallic power were ever denied. They were on display at the Louvre, if only shrivelled and of cold marble. Every now and then they popped out as threats, not sources of pleasure. My first re-membered sight of a penis was by courtesy of an immaculate besuited young gentleman, with neat French beard, who leapt into a courtyard off rue Soufflot as Margaret and I descended some stairs towards him. He shook his floppy implement and fixed us with an empty stare. I was numbed. Margaret, thanks to her parents' relaxed approach to nudity, dismissed him with an angry sweep of her hand. The gentleman withdrew. De Beauvoir's adolescent experience of gropers and flashers described in her *Memoirs* (p. 161) seemed more relevant to me in those days than her psychoanalytical discussions in *The Second Sex*.

Later feminists have, like de Beauvoir, attempted to confront in various ways the symbolic power of the phallus (for example, Millett, 1970; Mitchell, 1974; Gilbert and Gubar, 1979). Some have contested de Beauvoir's received view of the invisibility of the female genitals by celebrating them in life and art (for example, Judy Chicago's *The Dinner Party*) and looking at the experience of other cultures (see Ardener, 1975).

Some later French feminist writers like Irigaray (1977) and Kristeva (1977) have used the female genitals or whole body as powerful sources for an apparently basic feminine identity. De Beauvoir would not be criticised by them for any suggestion of anatomical determinism as such, but instead she would be criticised for having 'internalised' the negation of the female anatomy. These writers lay even greater emphasis on anatomy or the 'essential nature' of the female body and have paradoxically evoked a sympathetic approach from de Beauvoir (Jardine, 1979).

Irigaray considers that there exists a hidden, essentially feminine sexuality which derives from the distinct female anatomy and the 'two lips' (1977, p. 65). Accordingly, women's anatomy gives them a unique erotic experience, and Irigaray builds a theory of language on this. Whereas masculine language has a unity because of the 'singularity' of the penis, for women there are always at least two meanings.

Irigaray and others have in turn been criticised for their 'biologism' by other feminists (Brown and Adams, 1979). Thus any traces of biologism in de Beauvoir would not necessarily be seen as grounds for rejection by such writers as Irigaray (see also Sayers, 1982, p. 169). Nonetheless, de Beauvoir's tendency towards anatomical determinism is ambivalent and contradicts her emphasis on social intervention.

De Beauvoir returns in her argument to the assertion that the penis is valued only because society says so and therefore contests a simplistic suggestion that anatomy is destiny (see also Mitchell, 1974).

In reality it is not an anatomical destiny that dictates the young girl's attitude . . . If its (the penis) value is retained . . . it is because the penis has become the symbol of virility which is socially valorised. In this matter the effect of education and surroundings is indeed immense. (*DS* II, p. 26)

The passivity which is considered part of the ideal 'feminine' woman is not a biological fact, she states, but is imposed by the woman's educators and by society. In this sense she rejects a biological explanation for any apparently fixed 'feminine' character, and is therefore not in tune with some recent radical feminists who support the notion of 'natural' and 'essential' female qualities across time and space.

When contrasting the upbringing of the young girl with the young boy, de Beauvoir gives a devastating description of the

little girl's fate. As de Beauvoir moves towards the girl's experience of puberty, menstruation and sexual awareness, the evidence becomes more specific, although disguised as universal.
There are illuminating examples from literature, including that of
Carson McCullers, but there are also traces of her own experience. The description of a father's reaction to the daughter's first
menstruation (*2nd S*, p. 337) echoes evidence from the *Memoirs*.
The constraints on bodily movement recall her own. Again there
is the tendency, despite her formal denial, to present the girl's
responses as universal and therefore programmed by biology or
some innate psychology.

After each menstruation, the young girl is alleged to feel 'the
same disgust at this flat and stagnant odour . . . of the swamp,
and of wilted violets' (*2nd S*, pp. 337–8). De Beauvoir explains an
adolescent girl's sado-masochistic practices as a way of dealing
with this disgust at menstruation and the thought of adult sex.
She does not consider that these practices could as well be the
sublimation of desires. At other times the young girl escapes into
solitude; she becomes 'intoxicated with her isolation' and sees
herself as 'different, superior, exceptional'. She makes a promise
that her future 'will be a revenge upon the mediocrity of her
present life' (*2nd S*, p. 364). There was certainly autobiographical authenticity in this isolation, possibly a state shared by some of
her readers in the 1950s and early 1960s. I once vigorously
underlined this theme.

An extremely phallocentric view of male sexuality is presented.
Apparently the experience of male puberty is relatively simple.
Erotic desire is not realised within the young man himself but is
projected outwards. 'The erection is the expression of this need
. . . he projects himself toward the other without losing his
autonomy; the feminine flesh is for him a prey' (*DS* II, p. 130).
Although de Beauvoir argued earlier that the significance of
the penis/phallus has its origins in the social context, here she
has 'internalised' the primacy of the penis/phallus for man's
eroticism.

De Beauvoir offers descriptions of the differing social constraints or freedoms permitted to young girls and boys. She does
not consider that these differences would both reflect and reinforce each gender's subsequent attitude to their sexuality. A

languid sensuality of the whole body may be culturally repressed. In her discussion of *The Nude Male* (1979), Margaret Walters shows how the ideal in western art depicts the adult male nude as lacking receptive sensuality. If ever passive, the male nude must be heroic in pain, pierced with nails and arrows. Sometimes the active, whole body is portrayed as a giant phallus. These representations are culturally specific and not necessarily a picture of the innate and universal. Evidence from prostitutes reveals that male clients often seek passive, sensual roles. Men in trusting relations may learn that their repressed desires for languorous sensuality and passive, receptive postures may be nothing to be ashamed of. With life experience, I can make these observations, but as young virgin I was dependent on the public representations of male sexuality which de Beauvoir unwittingly reflected.

The view of the woman as passive prey in sexual intercourse is confirmed as follows:

It is through the vagina that the woman is penetrated and fertilised, it only becomes an erotic centre by the intervention of the male and that always constitutes a kind of rape. (*DS* II, p. 130)

Not yet having been initiated, and deferential to the mother/ author and initiator, I underlined that sentence.

De Beauvoir later said that she was wrong to suggest that a girl's defloration was always felt as such and dissociated herself from the more generalised view that sexual intercourse was a rape on each occasion. She was 'shocked' at such an assertion: 'When one says that intercourse is rape, basically one is adopting male myths. That would mean that the male sex organ really is a sword, a weapon' (Schwarzer, 1984, p. 36).

De Beauvoir was herself the recipient of male myths, and some peculiarly close to those of her own initiator and lover, Sartre. Whereas the preceding description of the female sexual organs presents them as near invisible, her subsequent metaphors are vivid and grotesque. Her own disgust, disguised as a universal, combines with Sartre's antipathy towards the raw and viscous, something which de Beauvoir was to recognise as peculiar to him and consistent with his 'refusal of all bodily passivity' (*Adieux*, pp. 315–17 & 334).

The female sexual desire is like the soft palpitation of the mollusc. While man has impetuosity, woman has only impatience; her expectation can be intense without ceasing to be passive; man dives upon his prey like the eagle and the hawk; woman waits like the carnivorous plant, the marshes in which insects and children are swallowed up. She is absorption, suction, vent hole, humus, pitch and glue, a still summons, insinuating and viscous. (*DS* II, p. 148)

The chapter on sexual initiation ends with pleas for mutual generosity, reciprocity and an end to the conditions which perpetuate women's inhibitions, all of which I vigorously underlined. Thus de Beauvoir's apparent message that a girl's sexual disgust with herself was somehow innate was not always read that way. There were in any case instances where the female reader might not see her own experience; for example, I did not see menstruation as the revolting thing she described; it was a joyful blossoming into womanhood and possible fertility in those early days. Our reading was selective, for there was sufficient material into which we could read our own conditions and de Beauvoir's polemic invited us to change them.

The passages on heterosexual relations were treated as textbook information to cloistered middle-class girls, if not to others. The public taboo against pre-marital sex in that epoch was accompanied by greater censorship of film and print. *Lady Chatterley's Lover*, the works of Burroughs and Miller were still banned in Britain in the early 1960s – something which feminists might now see as a mixed blessing. Both the pornographic and less exploitative publications were unavailable. The mood was one of secrecy and repression. The public discussion of sexuality in schools was confined to animal reproduction; that of human sexuality was reserved for medical experts. When confronted with a woman's text, some readers took de Beauvoir's descriptions of sexual intercourse as the truth and as future guide. My double or triple ink lines agree with the most questionable assertions . . . for example, that after intercourse the man becomes an integrated body, separate and preoccupied with the mundane – 'he wants to sleep, take a bath, smoke a cigarette, go out in the fresh air' – while the woman apparently wants to prolong the carnal contact (*DS* II, p. 162; *2nd S*, p. 417). Subsequent life experience and more public discussion deny these observations, which merely reflected de Beauvoir's own. De Beauvoir was considered especially outrageous by her critics for having discussed lesbianism, and although some of her uninformed readers considered that she had, however clumsily, 'normalised' lesbianism, her discussion is inadequate and sometimes a caricature of relations between women. For example, de Beauvoir reiterates some of the stereotypes of 'butch' or 'male' roles in lesbian couples. In those days, the subject was so taboo that, despite or because of my previous residence in a single-sex boarding school, not one word is underlined of that chapter.

The second section, 'Situation', deals with the circumstances and roles allotted to adult women, usually in terms of their relationship with men: for example, the married woman, the mother, the prostitute and the mistress. De Beauvoir's autobiographies again reveal the first-hand sources for her descriptions of these different adult experiences of women. In the case of the wife or the kept mistress, she writes from observations of other women in her circle. The polemic and value judgements do, however, come from a personal stance; her rejection of marriage, maternity, housework and the role of economically and emotionally dependent mistress. De Beauvoir's details about marriage find echoes in her observed experience of her mother, but again this is not made explicit. In the subsequent book about her mother she reveals: 'Her case alone would be enough to convince me that bourgeois marriage is an unnatural institution' (*VED*, p. 32). Her lengthy discussion of abortion, as opposed to childbirth, at the opening of the chapter on 'The Mother' continues to provoke anger. This was indeed her experience of conception. Years later, in the 1970s, she joined a public demonstration composed entirely of women who confessed to having had an illegal abortion.

The third section, 'Justifications', includes examples of women who seem to be both victims and guilty of 'bad faith' by colluding in their subordinate state. They are the 'narcissist', 'the woman in love' and the 'mystic'. Some show the worst excesses of masochistic self-denial or deluded self-adoration. There are some individuals in her autobiographies, especially Louise, apparently maddened by love (*PL*, pp. 167–79), who reappear in different guises throughout her work, whether as a general 'type' in *The Second Sex* or as a character in her fiction (Paula in *The Mandarins*, for example). The theme of the rejected mistress, mad and masochistic, in these three forms – in documentation, theory or fiction – worked best for some novice feminists like myself as a general, theoretical category in *The Second Sex*. If left only in her autobiography or fiction, these women might have appeared merely as chance individuals, without any import for the study of women in general.

This possibility is confirmed by the contrasting attitude of a middle-class white woman of my generation. Whereas she devoured de Beauvoir's early novels and autobiographies, she deliberately avoided *The Second Sex*, not because it was heavy going, but because she wanted to distance herself from any generalised theories about women. She could not accept any overall description of women's subordination. Instead, she preferred to identify herself with de Beauvoir's individual examples of a 'free', intellectual woman: Françoise in *She Came to Stay* or Anne in *The Mandarins*. In this way, she distanced herself from the 'failed' middle-class women whom she saw around her, and continued for a time to believe that women could achieve anything through individual effort. Today, she rejects this type of analysis.

The final section of Volume II, 'Towards Liberation', devotes considerable space to de Beauvoir's notion of the independent woman and provides the inspiring alternative to the preceding degraded and depressing pictures of women. Its positive inspiration, like other sections, is still not separate from a forceful description of ways in which women's independence is suppressed. At the outset, de Beauvoir declares that the

> kept woman – wife or courtesan – is not enfranchised of the male because she has in her hands a ballot sheet . . . She still remains in the position of vassal . . . it is through work alone that she is guaranteed concrete liberty. (*DS* II, p. 521)

Here de Beauvoir makes the mistake of overlooking unpaid domestic labour and defining work as only that which is paid. She also underestimates the servitude of most women's external employment. Here, in contrast to the preceding sections, de

Beauvoir focuses explicitly rather than covertly on the condition of the middle-class woman, with or without a career. The connection between her observations and her own position is less ambiguous. Again, her autobiography reveals some of her sources. The conflicting pressures and problems facing a woman are minutely documented: for example, the demands of outward conformity to a masculine model within the workplace, the pressures to hide intelligence and determination behind a 'feminine' mask, the restrictions on 'sexual adventures' and the incompatibility between a career and marriage or a long-term partnership. The woman is still expected to be 'a true woman . . . a good housekeeper, a devoted mother such as wives traditionally are' (*2nd S*, p. 703). Since de Beauvoir is herself an unusually privileged example of independence, her evidence and polemic here can only be relevant to a minority of women at the apex of a western class hierarchy. For it is still the case that the external employment which de Beauvoir advocated for all women would, for the majority, mean wage labour in exploitative conditions rather than a fulfilling 'career'.

In the section on independence, de Beauvoir exposes most clearly the reasons for her stand against maternity:

There is one feminine function that is actually almost impossible to perform in complete liberty. It is maternity . . . having a child is enough to paralyse a woman's activity entirely; she can go on working only if she abandons it to relatives, friends, or servants. (*2nd S*, p. 705)

Thus her biologically based description of maternity (in the opening pages of Volume I) which weighs a woman to the earth, and roots her in immanence because she merely maintains the species, is implicitly modified here by de Beauvoir's description of a specific context. If the problems of maternity can be explained by the *social* organisation of child care rather than by innate biological differences, then they are also amenable to change.

A younger generation of feminists will recoil from the negative view of motherhood. The section on the independent woman may be dismissed because it is concerned with the dilemmas faced by a middle-class woman who has chosen to reject maternity. De Beauvoir did not adequately explore any suggestion that men

116 *Simone de Beauvoir*

should share child care. Whereas in the 1950s and 1960s rejection of or delay in maternity was identified by some middle-class women as a feminist stance, today maternity is explicitly reintegrated within feminism, although it may not be easier in practice.

This second volume of *The Second Sex* still offers a rich ethnography of some women's experience. Many of de Beauvoir's observations continue to touch upon key questions even in changed times. Some aspects have subsequently become the subject for specialised studies; for example, a girl's education, female sexuality, marriage, maternity, housework, prostitution and romantic love. De Beauvoir's concluding discussion on the independent woman affirms that this ideal state is as yet impossible, but she does discuss the kind of equality which liberation should entail. It is interesting to see how she attempted such liberation in her own life.

Notes

1 Parshley translates the word 'collectivement' as 'in a general view', thus losing de Beauvoir's implicit links with Durkheim's and Jung's notions of collective ideas and myths.
2 These include *Thinking about Women* by M. Ellmann (1968) and *Sexual Politics* by K. Millett (1970).
3 See *Writing and Sexual Difference* edited by E. Abel (1984) and *Becoming a Heroine* by R. Brownstein (1984).
4 Some examples include; *The Female Imagination* by P. Spacks (1975), *Literary Women* by E. Moers (1977), *A Literature of Their Own* by E. Showalter (1977), *The Madwoman in the Attic* edited by S. Gilbert and S. Gubar (1979) and *Women Writing and Writing about Women* edited by M. Jacobus (1979).
5 See Jacobus on the writing of George Eliot in E. Abel (1984).

CHAPTER FIVE

THE PIONEER IN PRACTICE

De Beauvoir's volumes of autobiography only partially fulfil the 'correct' critical canon for an autobiography. Jelinek (1980) suggests that in fact these conventions are more likely to be associated with men's autobiographies, which tend to depict a chronological success story of public career and life progression. Such autobiographies which emphasise a linear career are likely to be middle class rather than working class. Women's autobiographies tend to be episodic and fragmented rather than chronological. They may then be misjudged as unstructured. The text is often marked by internal dialogue, self-doubt and the need 'to convince the readers of their self-worth' (*ibid.*, p. 15). Women's autobiographies tend to be more like personal diaries, not written as a record of public achievement for a congratulatory audience.

The autobiographies of de Beauvoir's adulthood are testimony to a mixed triumph. Whereas de Beauvoir depicts failed, dependent women in her fiction, she attempts to present the account of her life as an unmitigated success (Walters, 1976). This is only partially effective. The second volume, *The Prime of Life*, commences in a somewhat predictable female fashion with self-criticism and an apology for the restricted and misguided political views of herself and Sartre before the war. De Beauvoir declares that she and Sartre were mistaken in not having read more of Marx and Freud in that pre-war period, suggesting that these writers could have helped them out of an intellectual impasse.

Neither can the account of her personal life, specifically her relationship with Sartre, be read as an unproblematic success, despite its apparent innovative aspects compared to a bourgeois marriage. A close reading of her text reveals profound conflicts between her intellectual or emotional dependence on him, and her struggle for freedom.

Most of the volumes fit the supposedly male tradition in that they depict an accumulative public success, in de Beauvoir's case as a writer and intellectual in a country which gives supreme recognition to these roles. Chronology is obeyed only in broad phases; dates and exact details are generally ignored. The later volume, *When All is Said and Done (Tout Compte Fait)*, adopts a thematic rather than chronological approach. A recent critique of de Beauvoir's adult autobiographies is in line with the orthodox literary canon in that major emphasis is placed on structure, balance and even 'objectivity' or political 'impartiality', most of which are found to be lacking (Keefe, 1984). If this is the critical orthodoxy, then it would seem to undermine and contradict the very force of autobiography which, like no other writing, exploits subjectivity and one person's experience of history. Keefe prefers the earlier volumes, in which de Beauvoir has used the larger time gap between the experience and writing to help to create 'distance'. The adult autobiographies are indeed impersonal and detached in many aspects. This is in effect a weakness: 'Her catalogue of books and films and conversations often reads like an evasion' (Walters, 1976, p. 370). De Beauvoir's impersonal tone in describing aspects even of herself is consistent with her rejection of any psychoanalytical dimension. The unconscious does not exist for existentialism; the mind and emotions are open only to reasoned analysis. Whereas de Beauvoir is congratulated for her general 'sincerity' by Keefe, this quality is largely irrelevant when the reader seeks an analysis of the self's hidden undercurrents, which sincerity may often work to conceal.

Autobiographies never fulfil the ideal of self-revelation in practice; there are always major omissions. De Beauvoir's omissions are therefore not unusual. And there are many: key individuals in Sartre's and her life do not appear – for example, Sartre's adopted daughter. Whereas there is considerable candour in the *Memoirs*, de Beauvoir is conspicuously silent about her sexuality in relationships. Today she says that she regrets not having written more on this subject.

I would have liked to have given a frank and balanced account of my own sexuality. A truly sincere one, from a feminist point of view; I would like to tell women about my life in terms of my own sexuality because it is not just a personal matter but a political one too. I did not write about it at the time because I did not appreciate the importance of this question, nor the need for personal honesty. (Schwarzer, 1984, pp. 84–5)

Given the constraints of the times and the furore over her impersonal discussion of sexuality in *The Second Sex*, de Beauvoir had little choice (Mauriac wrote to a contributor to *Les Temps Modernes*: 'Your employer's vagina has no secrets for me' (*F Ci*, p. 197).) She and Sartre, as public figures, would be extremely vulnerable to yet greater invasions of privacy. Instead, the reader is left to decipher the covert autobiographical allusions in Volume II of *The Second Sex* and in passages of *The Mandarins*.

That de Beauvoir is insufficiently revelatory is a criticism which could as well be applied to the vast majority of the celebrated autobiographies of male success, which often give only a glimmer of personal relationships. It is also forgotten how scandalous to many or inspiring to us young women it then seemed for a woman merely to formalise in print the fact of her open and unmarried relationship. A century earlier, George Eliot could never admit publicly to living with a man outside wedlock. By contrast, in both centuries a man's public reference to mistresses would be in tune with the conventional double standard of morality for males. Given the criticism of de Beauvoir, it should be recognised that Sartre's projected autobiography shows even greater restraint; his single volume *Words* ended in adolescence. His posthumously published letters and diaries have the advantage of immediacy and intimate revelation (1983, 1984).

De Beauvoir's narrative of apparent accumulative success is dramatically broken at the end of the third volume, *The Force of Circumstance*, when she expresses disillusionment. The final words declaring that she had 'been swindled' were misread solely as a statement on ageing, but as she later explained:

It was not the outcome of seeing my own reflection in the glass but of my deep distress, my revolt at the horror of the world. When I compared this state of mind with my adolescent dreams, I saw how those dreams had led one astray . . . Bourgeois culture is a promise: it is the promise of a world that makes sense, a world whose good things may be enjoyed with a clear conscience; a world that guarantees sure and certain values. (*ASD*, p. 132)

De Beauvoir had the audacity to turn her success upside down and to argue its contradictions. She recognised her own initial privileges, the exploitation around her, the personal inability to change it and her class isolation.

I know that I am a profiteer, and that I am one primarily because of the education I received . . . I exploit no one directly; but the people who buy my books are all beneficiaries of an economy founded upon exploitation. I am an accomplice of an economy founded upon exploitation and compromised by this connection; that is the reason why living with the Algerian war was like experiencing a personal tragedy . . . the only solution would be to change the whole world, and I don't have that power . . . the consequence of my attitude is that I live in what approaches isolation; my objective condition cuts me off from the proletariat. (*F Ci*, pp. 668–9)

Added to this was de Beauvoir's resentment at her ageing, which shook any complacency in her readers and outraged critics of varied persuasions. Perhaps they had grown accustomed to the absence in acceptable autobiography of disruptive descriptions of painful experience.

In presenting her personal life as text for public gaze alongside impersonal essays and fiction, de Beauvoir invites outsiders to make a detailed analysis of her conduct and of her changing views at each stage. The reader may demand more than she is prepared to offer. Here, the adult autobiographies are found wanting compared to the *Memoirs*. Moreover, in writing the *Memoirs*, de Beauvoir drew on detailed diaries and she allowed her memories free imaginative rein. Whereas naïvety in childhood and adolescence is forgiven, indeed adds piquancy, in adulthood it will not be read as merely a phase. The adult autobiographies, on the other hand, were largely constructed without the aid of intimate diaries which, in adulthood, de Beauvoir wrote only at odd intervals, and then with minimum self-analysis.

In the later volumes, in order to recapture the past, she draws on newspapers scrutinised in libraries. Her adult life is portrayed within events selected by journalists, yet without the thematic overview of an historian. It is unclear whether de Beauvoir ever read the newspapers contemporaneously with the events she later recreates. In some instances she confesses to having ignored them at the time. The later autobiographies thus slide between a contrived documentation and lived experience. The public events portrayed may be just archival products. Sometimes the facts are wrong, not because she so experienced them but because she has to rely on others' evidence.

The journalistic reconstruction becomes more pronounced as the volumes progress. A woman of my generation who had avidly read the first two volumes of de Beauvoir's autobiography and responded to the similarities in her experience and descriptions of the self abandoned reading her altogether after the third volume. Although deeply affected by the description of French torture in Algeria, she sensed the inadequacy of the journalistic reconstruction. In the flyleaf she wrote:

a simple day to day narration of events in her life, interesting but much of this one could get from a newspaper anyway. What one wants to know are the ideas, preoccupations – a re-examination of their political beliefs, preoccupations about death etc . . . superficial and egocentric.

De Beauvoir's apparent egocentricism actually prevented a deeper examination of the self (see also Walters, 1976). The use of journalistic documentation reflects a need to make sense of her life in terms of external political events, a compensation perhaps for past naïvety and privileged isolation. The most memorable events as described in the autobiographies are those in which the reader can recognise the author as active participant; for example, de Beauvoir's experience of the evacuation from Paris. During her travels, other countries are also conveyed with unique insights when she is her *own* journalist.

Another concern for de Beauvoir is her self-assumed role as a chronicler of Sartre's intellectual development. De Beauvoir's autobiographies are in part biographies of her companion and have been used as such by Sartre's devotees. It is not clear whether de Beauvoir records each nuance in Sartre's thinking because he is a 'great thinker' at her side, like Boswell to Johnson, or because the record throws light on her own theories which, as abstractions, she agrees owe much to him. De Beauvoir makes no apology for deferring to Sartre's theories nor for hanging her material on the coat hangers of his concepts. In this sense Sartre's intellectual history becomes her own.

The adult autobiographies are not the place for self-probing. Despite the audacious confessions of jealousy and political short-comings as well as critical cameos of individuals, there is no attempt to unravel and then reconstruct the depth of her or her companion's emotions, inner flaws and irrationalities. In the years portrayed in *The Prime of Life*, both de Beauvoir and Sartre have breakdowns of a sort; these are described, along with some of the circumstances, as mere interludes. Both recover to reassert the power of reason over matter and emotion. In this sense, de Beauvoir's 'I' of the adult autobiographies is the rational actor and intellectual who seeks to repress and control any underlying contradictions in the self. In the preface to the third volume there is a sense that a motive behind the writing of her autobiography is the desire to control others' independent view:

I prefer rummaging through my past to leaving the task to others . . . Perhaps my image projected in a different world – that of the psychoanalysts – might disconcert or embarrass me. But so long as it is I who paint my own portrait, nothing daunts me. (*F Ci*, pp. 6–7)

In 1982 she acknowledged her reluctance to 'delve' into herself too much: 'I don't apply my analyses to myself all that often. It is not in my nature' (Schwarzer, 1984, p. 111).

As in her novels, women, including herself, are presented in terms of their rapport with men. In the major adult autobiographies the unitary thread, with the exception of the book on her mother, is her relationship with Sartre. By contrast, members of her own sex have generally minor parts. Early on, the new women in de Beauvoir's life are encountered through Sartre. De Beauvoir meets few on her own account. They are thus seen in terms of her relationship with Sartre. We read in detail of her jealousy of his former mistress, Camille. With one or two excep-tions, the women de Beauvoir meets independently of Sartre, such as her teacher-colleagues, are despised or ridiculed. One especially brutal example is that of the woman who made loving, sexual overtures to her. Her pupil, Olga, whom she rescues from the provinces and to whom she acted as mentor, is eventually drawn into Sartre's orbit.

There are glimpses in the autobiographies of the women who provided the concrete material both for *The Second Sex* and for her novels. De Beauvoir and her friends, she says, enjoyed observing others, especially in café society. There are strict class limits to that observation: there are no individual portraits of women or men from the working class and peasantry, not even the waiters or concierges who serve these Parisian intellectuals. When individual women are named, there is an unthinking focus on their physical appearance and public sexuality. The men are presented without physical description, they are disembodied; we hear more of their views, their minds and characters, but their wives or mistresses are conjured up as physical images – their hairstyles and dress are closely scrutinised and their beauty or ugliness is subjected to conventional judgements. Women become appearances, men are actors in the world:

Madame Lemaire was wearing a green tussore dress and a perky little hat to match: I had never seen her looking younger. Pagniez was wearing his most irresistible smile; I felt he was capable of turning everything he touched into sheer delight. (*PL*, p. 113)

Women as ornaments are assessed in de Beauvoir's account as possible rivals. Thus de Beauvoir sees women through a male gaze, and is later victim of her own gaze:

I often stop, flabbergasted, at the sight of this incredible thing that serves me as a face . . . While I was able to look at my face without displeasure I gave it no thought, it could look after itself . . . I loathe my appearance now: the eyebrows slipping down towards the eyes, the bags underneath, the excessive fullness of the cheeks, and that air of sadness around the mouth that wrinkles always bring. (*F Ci*, p. 672)

The autobiographies were written after *The Second Sex* but before a movement which alerted women to the implications of describing women as visual objects. In addition, by 1970, de Beauvoir was to confront ageing in a documentary study, *Old Age* (*La Vieillesse*, 1970), with a format echoing *The Second Sex*. As in the case of women, de Beauvoir suggests that the aged are treated as 'the Other'. She looks at the biological, psychological, economic and social explanations for the position of the aged. It fails in part because of its over-dependence on scattered documentation without the concealed, first-hand ethnography of her study of women.

As with the *Memoirs*, only a few aspects of the later autobiographies can be selected for discussion in this overview of de Beauvoir. The extent to which her adolescent desire for autonomy could be fulfilled is a key question. The early pattern of her relationship with Sartre and the experience of rivals for his attention are explored. Some of her emotional conflicts are projected onto her fiction. Her political practice is also a major subject for scrutiny. There are changes in de Beauvoir's continuing struggle for some kind of freedom. Her academic graduation coincides with the start of her lifelong connection with Sartre and its implications for other relationships and other ways of being. Political events, like the German occupation of France and the subsequent Liberation, the Algerian independence struggle, the Vietnam War and the events of 1968, followed by the women's liberation movement, all drew her into political awareness, out of some naïvety or isolation. The women's movement, especially, changed her relationship with women and encouraged political action of a collective kind.

● Uncertain dependence

The title of the second volume of autobiography, *La Force de L'Age*, translated as *The Prime of Life*, suggests the confidence of experience, age and independence. It deals with de Beauvoir's adult years before and during the war. De Beauvoir is finally freed of all formal links with her background. She acquires a room of her own, albeit in her grandmother's house, but she is treated with the same independence as the other lodgers. 'To have a door that I could shut was still the height of bliss' (*PL*, p. 12). Any confinement now is privacy on her own terms. The break with the past is marked by a switch of allegiance and a new form of dependence: her relationship with Sartre. There are difficulties in this new life. After her academic triumph she senses an anti-climax and lack of direction. For the first time she is of course free of the demands of an external academic syllabus. There is a loss of confidence and little connection between her youthful aspirations and reality. She does not know what to do with her freedom.

In the opening pages, de Beauvoir exposes the myopia of her and Sartre's notions of freedom and willpower, which were in effect made possible by their bourgeois privileges, and which explain the easiness of their neglect of events leading to the Second World War. She confessed they were

wrong about almost everything . . . public affairs bored us. We counted on events turning out according to our wishes without any need for us to mix in them personally . . . At every level we failed to face the weight of reality, priding ourselves on what we called our 'radical freedom'. (*PL*, pp. 14–15)

De Beauvoir recognises retrospectively that she and Sartre should have seen the limits to this freedom. In the mid 1960s, I underlined her reference to their 'political blindness' and her critical self-judgement which confessed: 'we believed that we were pure consciousness' and 'pure will' (*FA*, p. 20). De Beauvoir as mentor was seen to have failings.

There is not the same scrutiny of the dynamics of her relationship with Sartre. She is content to describe him as her intellectual superior, while simultaneously recognising that women are underprivileged in intellectual training and in knowledge of the world. Whereas Sartre attached little importance to happiness, she depended on it – to such a degree that any extreme unhappiness would encourage her to consider suicide. She finds traditional 'masculine' qualities in Sartre to which she defers:

In my eyes, Sartre by the strength of his attitude, surpassed me. I admired him for holding his destiny in his hands alone; but far from feeling embarrassed by this, I found it comfortable to consider him of greater esteem than myself. (*FA*, p. 30)

De Beauvoir then freely recalls two individuals with whom she once achieved a basic understanding; Zaza now dead, and her father. She recalls the overwhelming joy when her father smiled at her and when she could tell herself that in some respects 'this man, superior to all others, belongs to me' (*FA*, p. 31). When chance came her way to form a close relationship, she confesses that it responded to a 'long founded need'. Despite a curious assertion that she and Sartre were equal because he was only three years older, she recognises a continuity with her childhood and her relationship with Sartre in that it is associated with parental, near patriarchal authority:

> I had such total confidence in him that he guaranteed me the absolute security that I had once found in my parents, or God. (*FA*, p. 31)

While considering that this dominant psychic hold over her is merely sentimental, de Beauvoir mistakenly thinks that there is objective material equality between herself and Sartre.

The extent of de Beauvoir's early dependence on Sartre as guide is revealed in the description of the two years after her 'agrégation' and before she moved to her teaching posts in Marseilles and then Rouen. At the outset, their similar qualifications have differing implications. De Beauvoir recognises that whereas her position is against the grain of the usual expectations of women, even of her class, that of Sartre was merely an inevitable route for a man. There is a contrasting experience of males and females when moving to a public adult world:

> It seemed miraculous to me that I had torn away from my past so that I was self sufficient and able to decide for myself. I had once and for all affirmed my autonomy, nothing would take it away from me. Sartre by contrast was only moving to a stage in his existence as a man and one which he had for long foreseen with disgust; he was about to lose the irresponsibility of his early youth, he was entering the detestable universe of adults. (*FA*, p. 26)

The same paragraph moves on to discuss Sartre's sexual and general need for a diversity of women, but there is no mention of de Beauvoir's own need. Sartre as a male would of course have to face other restrictions such as national service, but his progress to another stage in masculine adulthood would also have the trappings of public achievement. Indeed, Sartre turned apparent setbacks to his advantage. His spell in the army in 1939–40 produced a million written words (*War Diaries*, 1984, p. ix). Earlier, youthful pain of a personal sort at the hands of a slightly older woman had not deterred him. Instead, he consoled himself with the thought of some public triumph. During his earlier affair with Camille he wrote: 'You make me suffer, but I'll have the last laugh, because I am a great man' (*ibid.*, 1984, p. 74).

In her accounts, de Beauvoir repeatedly measures her ideas by comparison and contrast with those of Sartre, who does not do the same. Just as she argued in *The Second Sex*, she notes in her autobiography how women's position ensures that they are unable to 'attack the world at its roots'. She hoped to know and express things about the world but she never expected to be able to 'tear away its ultimate secrets through sheer brain power' (*FA*, p. 46). Yet her deference to Sartre compounds this apparent gender difference. That year after graduation she was too absorbed in the novelty of new experiences to devote time to philosophy: 'I limited myself to discussing Sartre's ideas' (*FA*, p. 46). Some of Sartre's theories, we are told, 'suited' her 'well' (*FA*, p. 50). Sartre eventually changed her long-held view of literature which was once diametrically opposed to his own (*FA*, p. 45), and so she turned away from fantasy literature, a kind which feminist writers are now developing with considerable success. Sartre favoured realism. Sartre steered her away from 'art films' to 'initiate' her into cowboy and detective films (*FA*, p. 53), as if such masculine genres should be considered improvements. De Beauvoir hovered between what she sees as a caprice in her own choice and the only apparent alternative which was direction from her male lover:

In my eyes the only time that mattered was that which I spent in Sartre's company; but in practice there were numerous times which I spent without him. I spent a large part of this reading in disordered fashion, according to Sartre's advice or my own caprice. (*FA*, pp. 55–6)

Sartre's psychic hold, amounting to a paternal succession, may explain her willingness and desire to submit to him as intellectual mentor. Here, my interpretation differs from that of Heilbrun (1979), who has presented de Beauvoir as someone who found an equal rather than a paternal mentor. She fails to recognise any paternalism in Sartre. My intention in accentuating de Beauvoir's dependence and sense of confusion at this stage in her life is neither to dismiss her nor to 'blame' her, but instead to indicate the continuing asymmetry of gender amongst even the most 'successful' women in the intelligentsia. De Beauvoir had gained supreme recognition in male-dominated academia but she remained unsure of her abilities. She was keen to recall that she was second to Sartre in the exams, but Sartre had actually failed the previous year. His advantage second time round was somehow overlooked. De Beauvoir seems to accept the formal hierarchy and both consciously and inadvertently gives evidence of her own subordination which she does not analyse. In some instances, de Beauvoir seems to fulfil much of the classic academic wife's role by supporting and embracing his ideas. This dependence is excused by de Beauvoir because men, she says, have greater grasp of the world. She does not examine critically the long-term intellectual consequences of her deference to Sartre's overview. Insofar as she accepted his theories, she then had to answer for their flaws, especially in *The Second Sex*. Sartre later stated that de Beauvoir was the person who understood and could elucidate best his ideas. He did not see any double edge to this apparent compliment (*Adieux*, 1984).

De Beauvoir certainly gained advantages from access to Sartre's coterie; it may have been more difficult to make social and intellectual contacts without this first attachment. She rightly despised the alternative, namely the traditional and ambiguous French role of salon hostess for which in any case she lacked the economic resources. Even the earlier Gertrude Stein, who as writer and wealthy patron held salons in Paris, was initially cushioned from social isolation as a single woman by first sharing a flat in Paris with her brother. De Beauvoir likewise required a male 'escort' to penetrate Parisian intellectual circles, the male dominance of which is shown in *The Prime of Life*. De Beauvoir at times comes to reflect the male perspective in treating the wives and mistresses as mere adjuncts. In practice, she also could not fully escape that same position as adjunct. Although she had broken free of certain conventions, for example pre-marital chastity, and had rejected marriage and religious dogma, yet she finds and chooses an intellectual partnership which retained some of the asymmetry of the institution of marriage. Sartre and then de Beauvoir jokingly described their relationship as 'morganatic' when in fact the word refers to marriages in which the wife alone gives up certain claims upon her husband. Generally de Beauvoir does not protest; she only partially recognises her position. It has been suggested that their decision neither to marry nor to have a child was for Sartre's convenience (Walters, 1976, p. 367). De Beauvoir explicitly suggests that a child would have added nothing to the completeness of their relationship, to which she gives supreme priority. She interprets Sartre's guidance as intellectual emancipation into a world from which she had once been debarred. Rather than writing off de Beauvoir's experience, the reader of today can learn from the ambiguities in her account and understand its limitations in context.

In those early years, de Beauvoir's loss of inner direction reaches a climax: 'Incapable of giving up anything, and hence of making any choice; I lost myself in a chaotic and delightful stew' (*FA*, p. 64). She embarked on a novel but with no idea what to write about. To create, she understands, entails a perspective on the world, but 'the brute presence of the world crushed me and I saw nothing: I had nothing to show' (*FA*, p. 64). Her way out was one which feminist literary critics have since recognised as a common pattern in women writers; namely the act of 'mimesis' or imitation of the literary canon (Jacobus, 1982). This approach, it has been argued, can be creatively subversive. De Beauvoir decided to imitate the writing of others, and more especially a genre of fantasy. It failed for her, partly because Sartre rejected that kind of literature as deceptive. She worked without conviction; the result bordered on parody. By 1930 she scribbled in a notebook: 'I cannot reconcile myself to living if there is no purpose in my life' and 'I have lost my pride – and that means I have lost everything' (*PL*, p. 60). She felt her life was too easy, the 'good pupil' in her was beginning to get impatient. She kept at her writing only because Sartre demanded 'imperiously' that she did so.

She recalled the major shock and lack of confidence generated by meeting Sartre's friends and compared it to the 'subjugation' and humbling she once felt in the presence of her girlfriend Zaza. In both cases she retained her peace of mind by obliterating herself. On this second occasion, she sees herself as having eventually become a 'parasite'. Her friend Herbaud accuses her of betraying the individualism he once admired in her, but worse still, Sartre warns her that she seems to have stopped thinking and that she risks becoming a 'domesticated woman' – like certain heroines who, after a struggle for independence, end up being merely a man's companion. Thus Sartre, as her mentor, is not seeking to domesticate her. In response to such criticism, de Beauvoir does not react as an autonomous being but instead she tries to please her man; she still cannot escape the gender dynamic of conventional heterosexual relationships: 'I was angry with myself that I had disappointed him' (*FA*, p. 66). She had mistakenly thought that having met Sartre she could not fail to fulfil herself. Thus the reader notices that the dynamics of personal relationships, especially between women and men, require continuous vigilance.

De Beauvoir explains how, at the time, this new fear of subordination had nothing, it seemed, to do with feminism; she gave little consideration to the subject. She did not think of herself as a 'woman', only as a person. It was on moral grounds alone that she rebelled against the 'degradation' of accepting a secondary position. In a footnote, she recognises that her problem arose *precisely* because she was a woman but at the time she saw it only in individual terms. What de Beauvoir does not recognise retrospectively is the contradiction in seeking a way to independence at the instigation of her male lover and guide, and in order to please him. Neither does she consider that the very power of Sartre's direction, along with his friends', may have helped to create her loss of confidence and autonomy. Indeed Sartre cruelly suggested that de Beauvoir should seek to imitate his former mistress, Camille. This hardly neutral example only exacerbated de Beauvoir's sense of inadequacy because it became confused with personal jealousy.

De Beauvoir intuitively sees the new problems of dependency in a relationship in the few words she scribbled at the time: 'I would like to learn again about solitude: it is so long since I have been alone' (*FA*, p. 81). Thus we find that in adulthood, not just in adolescence, a woman of that era, class and culture had to seek individual respite from a multi-faceted subordination by isolating herself, by choosing exile.

The independent escape from confusion came for de Beauvoir

in 1931 with her first teaching post 500 miles from Paris, in Marseilles, where she had to make her own life for a while. It was an escape which at first she saw as a cruel exile from Paris and Sartre. Later she looks back on those early years in Paris as a warning of the near betrayal of youthful aspirations. Her arrival in Marseilles is marked forever as a turning point; she recalls standing at the top of a huge staircase:

I was there, alone . . . separated from my past and from all that I loved, and I gazed at the great unknown city where unaided, I would carve out my life, day by day. Up to then I had depended narrowly on others who had imposed limits and aims upon me. Now a great happiness had been given to me. Here I existed for no one . . . my actions, habits and pleasures were for me to decide. (*FA*, pp. 93–4)

Another liberation from the confusion of those early years came with de Beauvoir's extensive and lone mountain walks throughout the area surrounding Marseilles. Solitude as autonomy brought again a sense of power. These expeditions gave her 'solitary communion with nature and the feeling of private and individual freedom' (*PL*, p. 97). On her weekend breaks, de Beauvoir would walk up to twenty-five miles a day from dawn to nightfall, rejecting climbing boots and professional gadgets, preferring flimsy espadrilles and taking great risks:

I looked for a revelation from each successive hilltop or valley, and always the beauty of the landscape surpassed both my memories and my expectations . . . I rediscovered my mission to rescue things from oblivion . . . Alone again I got lost in a mountain ravine . . . Such moments, with all their warmth, tenderness and fury belong to me and no-one else. (*PL*, pp. 90–1).

On one occasion she refused to curtail her walk for the sake of her sister who came down with flu while accompanying her:

I refused, as I had done when twenty years old, to accept that life contained any wills other than my own.
 The will power that asserted itself in my fanatical walking trips had long established origins. (*FA*, p. 97)

Nature takes on a different significance from that experienced during her childhood holidays; it is no longer the site for erotic sublimation and release, but something to be overpowered. Open mountainous space is conquered with speed and muscular strength; there is little dawdling, little time for becoming one with the flora as in her childhood reveries. The body is subjugated to the will: 'I had never practised any sport, and so took all the more pleasure in making use of my body to the very limit of its potential' (*FA*, p. 97). Anne in *The Mandarins* shows a similar attitude.

The changes in de Beauvoir's attitude to nature followed her experience of sexual intercourse, with its more direct consummation of desire. When her lover, Sartre, went away on military service, and de Beauvoir was left alone with newly awakened desires, her body became a torment and an inconvenience:

Starved of its sustenance, it begged and pleaded with me: I found it repulsive. I was forced to admit a truth that I had been doing my best to conceal ever since adolescence: my physical appetites were greater than I wanted them to be. In the feverish caresses and love-making that bound me to the man of my choice I could discern the movements of my heart, my freedom as an individual. But that mood of solitary, languorous excitement cried out for anyone, regardless. (*PL*, p. 63)

She dared not confess such 'shameful' indiscriminate longings to Sartre. Later, in Marseilles, she was pleased that she had 'reconquered the peace of her body' (*FA*, p. 105). This was achieved, it seems, with the assistance of neither sexual intercourse nor masturbation. Reason and willpower reconquered her body whose uncontrolled sexuality was symbolised by the natural landscape over which she also triumphed.

In that open rural space there also lurked sexual threats outside herself. Her colleagues repeatedly warned de Beauvoir that she risked being raped on these solitary walks, but she dismissed their 'spinsters' obsessions', convincing herself that such things could not happen to *her*. One narrow escape merely confirmed for her that vigilance and decisiveness were sufficient. She did not regret having 'nursed this illusion for so long', since it gave her an important 'audacity' (*PL*, p. 94). It seemed she could acquire the illusion of female autonomy in that landscape.

● Violent emotions

De Beauvoir's reawakened and more solid independence in Marseilles did not shield her from all future loss of certainty. Solitude was no long-term solution and protection; it was merely an interlude. Personal relationships which compete with solitude cannot be subjected to simple rational controls. After de Beauvoir moved to a teaching post at Rouen, her relationship with Sartre was dramatically challenged by the entry of a third party, her pupil Olga. Although the unique aspects of any relationship in adulthood cannot be denied, I suggest that the experience was heightened because it echoed an experience from childhood. Here I offer an interpretation of de Beauvoir's own evidence which she herself makes no attempt to interpret.

Olga developed an increasingly intense, unconsummated relationship with Sartre to which de Beauvoir could not properly object, since she had agreed at the outset that Sartre could continue to have access to the 'seductive diversity' of women. Sartre explained to de Beauvoir in his favourite philosophical terms that their love was a 'necessary love' but that it would also be advisable for them to know 'contingent loves' (*FA*, pp. 26–7).

In practice this freedom was asymmetrical. Brought up to fear sexuality, de Beauvoir did not separate love from sex; thus contingent loves for her would be few. She could not automatically throw off her past. She rejected marriage but she found that she was 'not emancipated from all sexual taboos; women who were too easy or too free shocked me' (*FA*, p. 40). Thus she had internalised the double standard; one for women, another for Sartre and men. Even if she desired casual encounters, de Beauvoir was still subject to far greater social constraints than Sartre. Everything militated against a change in practice. For example, merely to be seen conversing with a male friend in Rouen stimulated punitive gossip among her teacher colleagues who also censored her classroom comments. De Beauvoir discusses these very problems in generalised form in the chapter on 'The Independent Woman' in *The Second Sex*. By contrast, Sartre could enhance his image in the company of a succession of beautiful young women. He used them to offset the feeling of his own ugliness. The publication of his letters to de Beauvoir and others reveals some of his orthodox attitudes towards women. He describes his sexual escapades and minute details of women's bodies to de Beauvoir, who is addressed as the voyeuristic collaborator:

Except for making love with her, I did *everything* with her . . . she is moreover delightful in bed. It's the first time that I've lain with a brunette or rather a *black* haired woman, as provençal as the devil, full of odours . . . She has solid thighs more enlarged below than above . . . very beautiful legs, a muscular and completely flat stomach and on the whole a supple and delightful body. (*Lettres au Castor*, July 1938, 1983, p. 188)

Sartre reports in a detached manner how the woman expressed jealousy of de Beauvoir rather than of his other mistress Tania, and then assures de Beauvoir that he remains united to her. Years later, de Beauvoir insists that this openness did not hurt her, but both she and Sartre admit to having hurt others (Schwarzer 1984, pp. 52–3).

More painful yet more concealed than the public asymmetry of gender was de Beauvoir's own intellectual and psychic dependence. De Beauvoir considered she had found a substitute for her father in Sartre. While she later rationalised her acceptance of the 'superior' Sartre in terms of unequal gender opportunities, long before she possessed such vocabulary she had in adolescence expressed a longing for a 'superior' man to 'lead her by the hand' through life (*MD*, p. 146). This adult mentor-protegée partnership was then threatened, not by Sartre's other lovers, but by the young Olga.

Clearly everyone may be subject to jealousy. But why did it take this specific form with de Beauvoir and why did the impasse have such a traumatic effect? A perspective from psychoanalysis is illuminating. When threatened by the younger Olga, de Beauvoir's reactions were twofold. First, she could be identifying with her former adolescent self and reliving the apparent triumph over her of Poupette for her father's attention (see Ch. 2). Simultaneously, another interpretation suggests that in her relationship with Sartre, at the level of *unconscious* fantasy, de Beauvoir had finally replaced her mother in 'father's' affections, as she had once longed to do in childhood. But then having become the mother figure, she is threatened by the entry of the 'daughter', Olga, with whom she had a maternal teacher role in real life. At the same time Olga is a reminder of her own past guilty self as young Simone, the daughter competing with her mother for the father's love.

The relationship between Olga, the younger woman, and Sartre, the partner/father, was apparently never consummated; neither of course were the analogous relationships between Simone's sister Poupette and Papa, and between Simone and Papa. Thus the Olga/Sartre pair reproduces aspects of her childhood. All would be well so long as de Beauvoir could be assured that the love with her partner Sartre remained the 'essential' one, in contrast to Sartre's 'contingent' loves. In childhood she had longed for an exclusive perhaps 'essential' relationship with Papa. Now as an adult she was re-living a childhood incestuous fantasy threatened by a rival.

The adult de Beauvoir found herself in a moral impasse. None of the reasoned discussion with Sartre about fairness and balance in their relationship could deal with the misplaced memories and thwarted desires of childhood. How could she object to the intrusion of Olga, if the latter unconsciously represented her younger sister, who in turn once threatened a tabooed fantasy between the young Simone and her father? Insofar as Olga represented her own guilty childhood self intruding upon the parental couple, she would recognise and unconsciously empathise with the younger girl's demand for gratification. But insofar as she identified herself with the mother in the trio, she would feel resentment for the daughter intruder.

If, as it seems from the evidence, de Beauvoir was indeed grappling with such uncontrollable yet conflicting feelings, this explains her impasse followed by hatred turned back on herself. On one level she resented Olga as a rival; on another, she felt it wrong to object because she would in effect be objecting to former incestuous fantasies in *herself*. As a way out, de Beauvoir succumbed to and nearly died of pneumonia. She recovered to transpose the trauma in the novel, *She Came to Stay* (1943).

In the autobiography, de Beauvoir does indeed suggest that she saw Olga as a 'child', with Sartre and herself as surrogate parents:

'a child up against an adult couple united by unfailing emotional bonds . . . it was we who controlled the actual destiny of the trio' (*PL*, p. 257). They had 'annexed' her. Gradually, de Beauvoir saw that Olga's influence on Sartre penetrated areas where de Beauvoir believed they had once been in firm agreement. When Olga disagreed with some of their cherished ideas, 'in the face of her opposition Sartre, too, let himself go, to the great detriment of his emotional stability, and experienced feelings of alarm, frenzy and ecstasy such as he had never known with me' (*PL*, p. 261). De Beauvoir's response, she said, went 'far beyond mere jealousy'. She began to ask if her happiness was all a huge lie.

In the novel, the de Beauvoir figure, the older woman, now Françoise, similarly sees the Olga figure, Xavière, as a child whose strong will is to be dominated (*SCS*, p. 26). She also sees that her partner, Pierre, the Sartre figure, succumbs to Xavière's 'childish whims'. Françoise considers that he 'had no right to change his opinion without warning her' (*SCS*, p. 48). Xavière's contrasting behaviour with Françoise and Pierre echoes de Beauvoir's description of her contrasting relationships with her father and mother (described years later in the *Memoirs*; see my Chapter 2). 'When alone with Françoise, Xavière, despite herself' allowed her feelings 'to be visible on a defenceless face, a child's face'. But with Pierre she 'felt herself a woman in front of a man and her features displayed precisely the shade of confidence or reserve she wanted to express' (*SCS*, p. 50). Françoise wonders 'how she could possibly have treated Xavière like an insignificant little girl' (*SCS*, p. 56).

In the novel, the dual and conflicting identification of de Beauvoir with her childhood self as daughter and her adult wish-fulfilment as mother is confirmed. But in her autobiography, she considers only that Françoise is a transposition of her adult relationship with Sartre and that Xavière is merely a version of Olga. Yet she also lets slip a clue from her unconscious: bracketed in passing, she appears not to see its symbolic implications: 'the character based on myself (I gave her my mother's name, Françoise)' (*PL*, p. 317). Her ambivalent portrayal of Xavière can be partly explained by her simultaneous identification with Xavière as the little girl, Simone, competing with her mother for Papa's exclusive love. Pierre is not only Sartre but also a memory of Papa. The name Pierre sounds like the French for father, *Père*. Pierre was 'the rock' on which she built her beliefs.

The response of de Beauvoir in real life, and of Françoise in the novel, to the threat of a female rival for a man's love follows a standard pattern in jealousy among women which is different from that among men (see Moi, 1982). When confronted by a male rival for the female partner, men's jealousy takes an aggressive, outgoing form and is directed more often at the unfaithful female rather than towards the male rival. When women are confronted by a female rival for their male partner, jealousy is often turned inwards and is depressive. If it does turn outward, the aggression is directed at the female rival rather than at the unfaithful male partner. Indeed all sorts of reasons are found by the woman for excusing her male partner's betrayal.

One reason for this lies in the different oedipal experience of male and female infant in being nursed by the female parent. These cannot be fully explored here (see Moi, 1982). Female fascination with and jealousy of the female rival expresses the ambivalent and pre-oedipal feelings of love and hate towards the mother. The jealous woman finds reason to forgive the male because, as in the oedipal/electra phase, she continues to idealise the father and finds satisfaction in continuing loyalty to him, while re-enacting aggression towards the mother as rival.

Part of de Beauvoir's and Françoise's pain is the recognition, albeit unarticulated, that Olga/Xavière's seduction of Sartre/Pierre/Père is the acting out of a desire she once entertained. In adulthood, she thought she had somehow finally fulfilled her heart's desire in choosing Sartre as mentor and sexual initiator. But the past is not buried. Unexpectedly, Sartre/Pierre responds to the childish spontaneity which failed ultimately to captivate her father and which she had had to learn to repress. In de Beauvoir's specific case, the apparent intellectual influence of the younger woman upon Sartre was all the more threatening since she had dutifully complied with what she considered his 'superior' intellectual power. Now someone else was captivating him by unseemly defiance.

The writer's work, de Beauvoir declares, is 'not to transcribe the emotions and thoughts which pass through you moment by moment but to point to those horizons which we never reach and scarcely perceive, but which nevertheless are there' (*FA*, p. 622). She also rightly insists that *She Came to Stay* is not a simplistic transcription of the events. We do indeed watch how her imagination is allowed to flow in fiction. Personal experience provided the base, but the use to which it is put is not subject to strict intellectual control. The competing forces of the unconscious surface in her fiction.

Sexual feelings in Françoise towards Xavière emerge (*SCS*, p. 246). This is also consistent with a specific pattern of female jealousy (see Moi, 1982). Whereas in her autobiography de Beauvoir makes no direct link between her personal torment and physiological collapse, when the events are transposed in the novel, she does indeed make the connection between her resulting depression and pneumonia. In fiction, the trauma is eventually dealt with in a revengeful manner; aggression is turned outwards to the female rival. Françoise sleeps with Xavière's male lover in order to hurt her. Then Françoise murders Xavière. De Beauvoir correctly states that Xavière is *not* a realistic description of Olga, she is partly fictional. De Beauvoir has in effect exaggerated and invented characteristics in Xavière, in accord with her very real fantasies. The figure which Olga represented for de Beauvoir in real life was also her own creation; Olga and Xavière are also her childhood self.

My argument that both the novel and the Sartre/Simone/Olga triangle are not free of de Beauvoir's earlier experience is confirmed by her revelation that the pattern had crystallised long *before* Olga came to be significant in her life (*PL*, p. 317). The only way out of her moral dependence on Sartre, she had thought, was to commit some crime to assert her independence. She imagined the appearance of an alien personality; 'through jealousy and envy I committed some crime which put me at this person's mercy, and achieved my own safety by destroying the Other' (*PL*, p. 316).

De Beauvoir's imagination and her fictional version of life do not escape their specific and material context nor her psychic past, although the novel was interpreted at the time as a primarily existentialist exploration of problems of individual existence when confronted by 'the Other', it was not, however, emphasised that this existentialist novel is gender specific. The 'Other' becomes the classic problem of 'the other woman' and de Beauvoir's resolution conforms to historically specific patterns of female jealousy. Françoise does not murder the male beloved, but the female rival. Thus any wish fulfilment in the novelist remains rooted in the female condition. The murder was precipitated by another act of revenge against Xavière by Françoise when she engaged in sexual relations with Xavière's young suitor Gerbert, and Pierre's protégé. This fictional liaison replicates that between de Beauvoir and Bost, which was concealed from Olga and approved by Sartre (Francis and Gontier, 1985, p. 176).

Both in the autobiography and in the novel, the actions of Sartre/Pierre in the triangle remain free of critical scrutiny. There is no attempt to unmask the historically specific power imbalance, despite the ample evidence, in both the autobiography and the novel, of asymmetry and self-deceptions disguised as open freedom. In the novel, Pierre senses Françoise's distress and offers to break off with Xavière. This honest chivalry makes it even more difficult for Françoise to object, for she in turn has been given freedom in love. But it is only abstract. Pierre's greater power in the world is not confronted. De Beauvoir explained that she did not present the 'I' of Pierre's story because, she said, he was so close to Sartre that she was reluctant to offer his portrait to the public. This again reveals a desire to protect him from blame through exposure. So closely did de Beauvoir identify with Françoise that she said that she could not envisage linking her with any other man, a stranger (*PL*, p. 342). Thus her loyalty to Sartre remained firm in fiction as in life.

In the novel, Pierre's greater power in contrast to Françoise is supported by objective material evidence. He is a celebrated theatrical director who enjoys couch casting his actresses. Françoise, by contrast, is an unpublished writer and therefore socially insignificant. Xavière soon recognises Pierre's superior power in the world and Françoise loses influence over her. This 'progression' from mother to father both reproduces de Beauvoir's childhood and Olga's relationship with de Beauvoir, her former school teacher. Pierre is *producing* a play about betrayal, *Julius Caesar*, and is not represented as the actor/traitor in the events around him. Soon Pierre decides to teach Xavière acting; he will draw her out, direct her. This again has resonances with the young Simone's image of her father. He was an enthusiastic amateur actor, and he once successfully directed her sister as 'Queen of the Night'. Pierre's relationship with Xavière is exploitative as an older man with power and experience. He seduces her with such glamour, but refuses to offer her more than a 'contingent love'. Xavière wants more than this. Instead of confronting Pierre's exploitative position, de Beauvoir, the author, attacks the rival woman who is also Pierre's victim.

The novel's denouement had a 'cathartic quality' for de Beauvoir. In destroying Olga on paper she 'purged' herself of all resentment of her (*PL*, p. 340). She believed the crime released Françoise from the dependency which her love of Pierre had induced, so that she could regain 'personal autonomy'. De Beauvoir is at pains to explain that the murder is not simply a capricious device to end the novel; she wrote it with tightened throat as if carrying 'the burden of a real murder' (*PL*, p. 340). She reports others' criticism of the conclusion as 'the weakest' part of the book and admits that she could not invest Xavière with sufficient 'malice and consistency' to arouse obsessional hatred in Françoise (*PL*, p. 339). This can be better explained by her incapacity to make her former adolescent self all bad. Nonetheless, she succeeds in killing off that past guilty self, as well as her rival, and in her mid thirties is thus freed to become a prolific and wide-ranging writer.

The theme of dependent women continued, however, to haunt her; they are fiercely documented in *The Second Sex* and in later novels, especially *The Mandarins* (1954) and *The Woman Destroyed* (1967). In *The Mandarins* elements of her own biography are again allowed creative exaggeration. The character Anne is made a psychoanalyst, whose theories in real life de Beauvoir rigidly avoided. Anne discovers through analysis;

> I had a rather pronounced Oedipus complex, which explains my marriage to a man twenty years my elder, a clear aggressiveness towards my mother, and some slight homosexual tendencies which conveniently disappeared . . . The ambivalent feelings I have in regard to my daughter stem from my aversion to my mother as much as to my indifference concerning myself. (1960, p. 39)

As this extract reveals problematic mother-daughter relationships are also a favourite theme in both these novels, and in *Les Belles Images* (1966) and in Volume II of *The Second Sex*. Still in the 1980s, de Beauvoir showed herself fixated on an imaginary mother-daughter antagonism and links it to her decision not to have a child (a rival for Sartre?):

I have never regretted not having children . . . When I consider the relationships the women I know have with their children, especially with their daughters, they often seem dreadful to me. I am genuinely glad to have escaped that. (Schwarzer, 1984, p. 54)

After creating a literary object external to herself, de Beauvoir seemed to have settled into an uneasy equilibrium with Sartre. Both reaffirmed the wish to resort only to 'contingent' loves which would not threaten their own relationship. In practice, other loves in Sartre's life risked becoming essential. When de Beauvoir was on a visit to the United States, Sartre asked de Beauvoir to prolong her absence from Paris so that he could spend more time with 'M'. De Beauvoir sought immediate consolation by seeking out an alternative partner – Nelson Algren, with whom she conducted a trans-Atlantic affair for a few years. De Beauvoir's anxiety about Sartre and 'M' later 'bordered on mental aberration' (*F C*i, p. 137) and she resorted to the drug orthedene. Sartre did not appear to have been threatened in the same way because de Beauvoir never sought a replacement for him. He wanted to be the central figure, even in his relations with other women:

Basically I didn't much care whether there was another man in an affair with any given woman. The essential was that I should come first. But the idea of a triangle in which there was me and another better-established man – that was a situation I couldn't bear. (*Adieux*, p. 304)

It is no accident that the two other men with whom de Beauvoir formed prolonged relationships could not be a realistic threat to Sartre. One was to be separated by space and culture, the other by age. Neither Nelson Algren in the States nor de Beauvoir were prepared to leave their respective countries to live together. De Beauvoir, it seemed, could only be fully 'unfaithful' to Sartre, her mentor, when outside her own culture, but even then she retained her primary loyalty to him, to Algren's bitterness (see Evans,

1985, pp. 41–3). The other man, Claude Lanzmann, many years younger than de Beauvoir, was a member of the Sartre entourage. In any case, 'the way his mind worked' reminded her of Sartre (*PL*, p. 264). Even when living with Lanzmann in the 1950s de Beauvoir spent regular periods working alongside Sartre in his apartment. Similarly, her earliest liaison, after the establishment of her relationship with Sartre, was with his star pupil, Bost (Francis and Gontier, 1985, p. 176).

In the early years in Paris, Sartre and de Beauvoir had always retained separate rooms in the same hotel and by the mid 1950s acquired their own apartments. Their sexual relationship ceased after twenty years (Schwarzer, 1984, p. 108). They continued to take their summer vacations together and in the later years went annually to Rome. Sartre sometimes spent separate vacations with his latest amour or brought her along as well. De Beauvoir makes little comment on these matters. We merely learn that sometimes she brought Lanzmann along, after having been on her own with Sartre. Although in the late 1940s, de Beauvoir made lecture tours in Spain and the States in her own right, in the 1950s and 1960s de Beauvoir accompanied Sartre, the major celebrity, on international visits to China, the USSR, Cuba, Brazil and Japan. She remained the continuous, possibly the pivotal, figure in Sartre's life, although Sartre continued to keep the company of younger lovers. As infirmity and poor eyesight overtook him, de Beauvoir, with the assistance of other women, assumed the major task of administering to his various practical and reading needs (*Adieux – A Farewell to Sartre*, 1984). Again there are parallels with the traditional wifely and female role. The question is whether Sartre would have done the same for her. No

● Isolation and political limitations

Like *The Second Sex* and the *Memoirs*, de Beauvoir's adult autobiographies were also something of an inspiration to some women of my generation and after. For some, the appeal was *precisely* that she kept company with mainly male intellectuals and that she legitimated the female intellectual. Some younger women today continue to find a model of achievement in de

Beauvoir's adult autobiographies. There was an added political dimension to her influence. De Beauvoir's account of her opposition to French colonialism in Algeria was encouraging to those women readers who were more responsive to a political critique from a woman.

My youthful reading of de Beauvoir's adult autobiography in the early 1960s did not extend beyond fifty pages of *La Force de L'Age* (*The Prime of Life*), which I commenced in the third year at my English University. The ink underlinings petered out and the pages remained uncut. *The Second Sex* and the *Memoirs* had, it seems, been the significant guides. *The Prime of Life* lacked the polemic of the one and the boundless optimism of the other.

The explanation for the loss of curiosity in pursuing de Beauvoir's life rests again on the potential for identification between female writer and reader. In the second volume, she had graduated academically, but in her self-description she was neither a political nor faultless feminist mentor. Having previously read her with total involvement, I continued to demand perfection of this sister/mother and now found her lacking. The ink underlinings in *La Force de L'Age* begin to follow multiple criteria. The consistency of the earlier ink marks has dissipated. In some instances, there is still identification between writer and reader, but increasingly, the ink marks highlight information from which the young woman reader is now personally and emotionally detached. The marks become a visual record of objective facts about French culture. The mid-sixties reader no longer privileges shared insights nor ones to imitate. But even in those later days, there was a limit to detachment; reading de Beauvoir as my female mentor could not easily be transformed into mere intellectual enterprise, nor could her autobiography be treated simply as archival sources in feminist history. So the autobiographies were abandoned. Nevertheless, I held fast to the personal lessons of earlier reading and carefully avoided any disturbing disillusionment.

The distancing between mentor and reader came with loss of synchronism. Two years earlier, I had echoed her apparent faith in the ideal couple with mutual intellectual interests. This had since been put to the test when I had fallen for a disarming beauty in socialist clothing. Romance was heightened by his arrest and sentence to a month's imprisonment for organising a CND march and non-payment of fine. I read, underlined, and sent him Stendhal's *The Charterhouse of Parma*, which recounted the love between a young woman and a prisoner. Did I imagine myself an 'authentic' heroine approved by de Beauvoir again? His letters spoke of love and of grandiose political aims. Having rejected his marriage proposal, I expected some partnership for a while. When he had asked if I could get used to his being famous one day, even then I was not impressed. Two weeks after his release and our being together, he abruptly told me not to touch, not to see him again. It was nothing to do with me as an individual, only as a type, for certain men were to repeat this pattern with numerous women, whom they deflowered with devotion and then threw away. Mental hospitals administered drugs to the rejects of such male idols whose political careers continued apace. For some men, in those times, socialism, even pacifism, masked a desire to win, degrade and torment the female sex. So much for my Sartre. It was not until the late sixties, the civil rights movement and the Vietnam war protests that women as a group recognised sinister contradictions in many men with supposedly egalitarian ideals (see Mitchell, 1971; Rowbotham, 1973). There are of course no such contradictions in men who support a class and race hierarchy where women are also seen as subordinate. Unlike socialists, these men need no egalitarian pretence.

This insertion of a fragment of the commentator's autobiography offsets the exposé of de Beauvoir's biography, especially her vulnerability to the 'law of the father', disguised as lover and intellectual partner. Self-exposure frees the commentator to scrutinise the other. Writing of a mother/mentor evokes ambivalent responses: admiration, the desire for emulation, alongside childish, daughterly resentment and fear of counter-attack and rejection by the mother. In Ascher's extended letter/chapter to de Beauvoir, she also treats her as the mother-writer with all of a daughter's ambivalence. Ascher recalls the 'combination of recognition, fear and anger' in her first reading of *The Second Sex* (1981, p. 110). During the writing of her tribute to de Beauvoir, the continuing 'frustration' in her response to her as a 'bad mother' was countered by a view of her as 'good':

the sternness which I sense from you in the day (so like my mother's) turned to 'kindness and support in my dream state'. (*ibid.*, p. 112)

De Beauvoir's example, even with her cultural and class privileges, demonstrates that women cannot by lone, individual endeavour escape the general conditions of subordination, material and psychic. De Beauvoir was for the most part free of the economic subordination of marriage, yet other dependencies remained, despite her denials. She struggled with her own confusion. For decades, de Beauvoir survived, it seems, without a female confidante comparable to Zaza. Until she met Sartre, her experiences of heterosexuality had been largely confined to the imagination. Her youthful grasp of the world, insofar as it was through books or fantasy, could not tell her how to participate; she had to learn through practice within the limits of the prevailing conditions. Similarly, de Beauvoir's own textual blueprint cannot save individual women from practical naïvety. Moreover, her text carries its own naïvety, both political and personal.

In my 1963 copy of *La Force de l'Age* there is a large question mark in the margin where de Beauvoir defers unquestioningly to Sartre's intellectual superiority and so appears to betray the authority of *The Second Sex*. Although earlier (*MD*) she used male privilege to rationalise her preference for a 'superior' male, she could have offered a different response, one which explored the alternative and subversive forms which a female intellect might take when contesting those male privileges.

At my English university of those times, the privileges attached to the male gender cut across those of class. Massive endowments in the all-male colleges ensured bursting libraries, subsidised meals and spacious studies. For every eight college places for men, there was one for a woman. In the early 1960s the total annual income for all the women's colleges was less than the price of one male college's new boat. The male tutors, with superior conditions for research and teaching, encouraged originality and daring in their all-male students, or so it appeared from outside (see also Sciama, 1981). It seemed, in this case from the inside, that the female tutors who had come up the hard way by deferring to rather than defying the phallic canon counselled caution and rewarded pedantry. In these circumstances, it would have been masochism to accept de Beauvoir's belief in any individual male's superior intellect; it depended on what was being assessed and by whom. The intellectual daring and freedom which we recognised and envied in male contemporaries did not lead to an under-estimation of women's qualities. Sometimes in so closely imitat-ing the male academic canon, they also subverted it through irony.

More significant than de Beauvoir's autobiography of gender relations was the political apologia at the opening of *La Force de l'Age*. Today its candour can be read as history. In the early 1960s I did not want to learn about her pre-war naïvety since socialist struggles had also been crucial in that earlier historical period. Later, de Beauvoir was to renounce her 'individualistic, anti-humanist way of life' and learn 'the value of solidarity' (*PL*, p. 359), but that was much later in her text.

In the mid 1960s, despite the conservatism of the university authorities and Macmillan's government, the student societies experienced a socialist renaissance. Despite the turgid politics syllabus, we were reading Marx, Luxembourg, Goldman, Trotsky, Nkrumah and Marcuse out of school hours. We marched from Aldermaston. We listened to Nelson Mandela and Bertrand Russell, and I spent a morning with Malcolm X. Each year, another colonised nation broke free. With Algeria's in-dependence, I pinned a speech on my wall by an Algerian woman calling also for women's freedom. All around were inspiring students from Africa and the Caribbean who offset the uptight American 'wasps'. My friend Katherine had been the first west-ern student to study in East Germany; another friend talked of Sharpeville and her family's expulsion from South Africa. This was not the time to pick over de Beauvoir's apologies for pre-war individualism. But this climate did explain the continuing hold of *The Second Sex*'s polemic among fragmented clusters of women. The very political ferment of the mid sixties which distanced the reader from de Beauvoir's confessions of general political naïvety was yet to lead back to her concern with gender, which was itself to be politicised.

If I had persisted in the mid sixties with the autobiography instead of giving up early into the second autobiographical volume *The Prime of Life*, de Beauvoir's description of the

German occupation of France and the Resistance movement would have been found to offer a focus for political discussion, and indeed was a major reason for the book's success when first published. Since the volume ended with the Liberation it conveyed 'an optimism' (*F Ci*, p. 595) which de Beauvoir realised, at the time of publication, had been short lived, given that French post-war socialism soon collapsed and that she was witnessing the repressive measures against the Algerian independence struggle.

Both then and today the volume can be read as a devastating lesson for the complacent academic or intellectual. Out of de Beauvoir's and Sartre's political naïvety came the notion of commitment or 'engagement' which through the post-war years they continued to refine. These questions were debated in Sartre's novels *The Road to Freedom*, and in de Beauvoir's *The Blood of Others* and *The Mandarins*. Many women, including myself, read the latter in the early sixties. My expectations of the novel were not the same as those of her autobiography; again the female reader became gender blind in relation to the characters. All of the women characters were clearly flawed as role models. This was deliberate on de Beauvoir's part. Anne pursues her profession 'with discretion; the axis of her life is the lives of others – her husband, her daughter'. Her 'dependency . . . relates to the majority of women' (*F Ci*, p. 276). The writer in the novel is made male because de Beauvoir wanted the reader.

to envisage him as a fellow being and not as an exotic animal; but a woman with a literary vocation is even more of an exceptional being than a man with that vocation. (*ibid.*, p. 276)

So the male characters more than the females seemed to be grappling with the significant political dilemmas. De Beauvoir chose to record the 'reality' of women's condition rather than to create a fictional woman who moved in the public political arena. Henri, especially, was the character with whom I found some identification. The ink underlinings sympathised with his dilemma as to whether he should immerse himself in economics or literature. There are many of de Beauvoir's own intellectual concerns written into Henri. Of this I was not then aware. As with other women readers, the gender significance of *The Mandarins* was that its author was female and that she communicated her privileged access to a left-wing intellectual clique. We admired de Beauvoir as author for this grasp of the public domain and for her 'masterly' portrait of powerful men. She transposed or disguised part of her own experience in the leading male, not just in the over-dependent character Anne. Thus de Beauvoir's actual political experience as a woman was so exceptional that she had to fictionalise it as male. The reality of her own social and political position had to be hidden, she thought, in order to make the book seem real.

Prior to the experience which was drawn upon for these political novels, de Beauvoir's interest in political commitment was, she claims, stimulated by Sartre. For both, the war exploded their individualism and to some extent tempered the notion of free choice. The arrest of Jews around them undermined any bland ideas about equal freedoms. Sartre's experience of national service and imprisonment brought him for the first time into intimate contact with members of the working class and, by 1940, he declared that he would no longer stand aloof from politics. He adopted the notion of 'authenticity': every man would have to take responsibility for his 'situation' and in order to transcend this, action was required. Anything else would be escapism or 'bad faith'.

De Beauvoir's diary of that time records:

It is clear that a real change had occurred in him and also in me as *I immediately rallied to his ideas*, for not so long ago our primary concern had been to keep our situation at a distance by games, diversions and lies. (*FA*, p. 442; my emphasis)

In a scholarly study of de Beauvoir's political theory and practice in relation to existentialism, Anne Whitmarsh concludes that the pattern for de Beauvoir's political position through to the 1980s, was set before the Second World War – at the time outlined above:

her life has exemplified with little change the remarkable persistence of the attitudes and values that had been established by the time the war broke out. (1981, p. 28)

These attitudes include de Beauvoir's opposition to the political right and the bourgeoisie, and her rejection of religion.

Her support for revolution has remained as strong as ever, but her political interest, awakened by the war, has only led to a minimum of action . . . Her pursuit of freedom . . . has become circumscribed. She began to realise that freedom was restricted by the presence of others . . . But she learned to fight just as passionately for the freedom of others as for her own. (1981, p. 28)

The war made her more aware of her links with others. Life was then seen as a 'compromise between herself and the world' although she now sought 'happiness through commitment to other people' (*ibid.*, p. 29).

Clearly, the extent of de Beauvoir's political activism has been affected by her simultaneous commitment to the solitary and sedentary practice of intellectual work. But this, Mary Evans has argued more recently, may have equally valid political consequences. Whitmarsh, Evans considers, is 'misguided' to suggest that:

politics are only about organised action and not about the written word, the critique of existing society . . . Many political movements, many changes . . . have taken place because of activity in the apparently remote and isolated academic's study. (Evans, 1985, p. 103)

Evans considers it more appropriate to look at the validity of de Beauvoir's political writing. In this she finds de Beauvoir lacking. For example, her programme for women does not take into account those women for whom paid work is 'far from emancipation', nor does she adequately consider the case of women who reject heterosexuality (*ibid.*, p. 106). Her analysis of the other countries she visits remains that of a traveller, merely passing through, and her belief in the 'redemptive power of education' is within a liberal tradition (*ibid.*, p. 69). De Beauvoir's political programme is, according to Evans, in these instances inadequately worked through.

Up to her mid sixties, de Beauvoir's notion of political action was somewhat constrained by male definitions. Anne Whitmarsh presents a detailed account of de Beauvoir's politics in terms of existentialist commitment, tracing her differences or similarities with Sartre and their changes over time (1981). Both moved from pre-war naïvety to committed participation within the Resistance and to socialism. De Beauvoir, in defining herself primarily as an intellectual, seemed content to remain 'incompetent' in the practicalities of direct action. Sabotage, for example, was left to others. Whitmarsh suggests that de Beauvoir 'accomplished a sense of action for herself through characters she created like Jean Blomart in *Le Sang des Autres*' (*The Blood of Others*) (1981, p. 130). But even though Blomart joins the workers on the factory floor, he can never become like them, he cannot jettison his middle-class past. Similarly, de Beauvoir felt herself justified in being unable to resort to practical action.

Already, before the war, she had distanced herself from the example of Simone Weil, another woman at the Ecole Normale, who had insisted on direct contact with the working class. Weil worked as a farm labourer in the university vacations, was involved in the trade union movement and taught at a working men's college. After some factory work, she joined the Spanish Civil War in 1936. De Beauvoir writes as if she is properly vindicated by her own non-participation in the Spanish Civil War:

There was a danger of being a nuisance rather than a help. Simone Weil had crossed the frontier determined to serve with the infantry; but when she asked for a gun they put her in the kitchens, where she spilt a bowl of boiling oil all over her feet. (*PL*, p. 290)

De Beauvoir enjoyed working in small groups, for example, that first devised by Sartre, 'Socialisme et Liberté', which aimed to disseminate information during the Resistance and to formulate a post-war socialism:

. . . we only had to be in each other's company to know that we were united, and to sense our joint strength. We agreed to remain leagued together in perpetuity against the systems and men and ideas that we condemned. (*PL*, p. 562)

As Whitmarsh suggests, the group also appealed to de Beauvoir because it was a literary activity and 'it took place behind the scenes' (1981, p. 99). De Beauvoir showed similar enthusiasm working on the post-war journal *Les Temps Modernes*. Despite her extensive experience of lecturing at universities, for example, in the United States, she tended to avoid public speaking at political gatherings. It is not clear whether this was due to nervousness or to a sense of detachment. She somewhat ingenuously justifies her absence from meetings such as the communist Comité National des Ecrivains (National Committee of Writers) in terms of her union with Sartre:

I was so completely in harmony with Sartre's views that my presence would simply have duplicated his, to no useful purpose. To go along struck me as both inopportune and ostentatious. It was not other people's malice I feared so much as my own embarrassment: I would have felt, in my inner heart, that I was making a tactless exhibition of myself. (*PL*, p. 563)

The latter part of this quotation reveals her self-consciousness at public gatherings, which also bored her. Whereas she had thrown herself 'heart and soul into "Socialism and Liberty"', because it was an improvised and hazardous undertaking', the CNE's sessions, from Sartre's account, 'had an official, indeed a routine, flavour about them which I found something less than attractive' (*PL*, p. 536). Her distaste for this kind of politics was continuous. As late as 1965 Sartre said of de Beauvoir:

There's only one matter on which she completely staggers me, and that's politics. She doesn't care a damn about it. Well, it's not exactly that she doesn't care, but she won't have anything to do with the sordid manoeuvres of politics. (Gobeil cited by Whitmarsh, 1981, p. 98)

Insofar as such politics with their bureaucratic agenda, hierarchies and legalistic procedures are male defined and male dominated, de Beauvoir's alienation, which took the form of boredom, is one shared by many women. The women's movement was to challenge not only the agenda and content of such political practices, but also their form. Consciousness-raising could take place only in the small group and after the jettisoning of formal procedures. It entailed self-exposure in an atmosphere of mutual trust and improvisation. Some of these characteristics of the movement were those which de Beauvoir had grabbed on to or found to be wanting in the past. There were other innovations in the women's movement. Mass meetings worked best for women when men were excluded, for it was soon found that even when men were in a minority, they acted as if they were the majority, intimidated diffident women speakers, and re-established the agenda on their own terms. De Beauvoir later supported the exclusion of men from women's meetings (Schwarzer, 1984, p. 34).

Before these experimental forms, de Beauvoir was confined to a more traditional political action. As a celebrated intellectual in France, she and Sartre were in a position to make pronouncements which had considerable impact in the public domain. In this sense their committed stance had greater significance than that of writers in other western nations where intellectuals are less fêted. Political commitment also took the form of participation at international conferences from the mid fifties; for example, the Congress of the World Peace Movement at Helsinki. But again she was bored with its endless speeches. She was later to travel as a celebrity, with political implications, in Eastern Europe and the Soviet Union, as well as in Latin America, Africa and the Middle East.

Whereas Sartre was sometimes close to joining the Communist Party, de Beauvoir maintained a greater distance. She could not bring herself to accept a total ideology and emphasised the value of individual freedom. The existentialist emphasis on individual choice could be seen as incompatible with a Marxist notion of the collectivity. De Beauvoir discussed these problems in her existentialist essay *Pour une Morale de l'Ambiguité* (*The Ethics of Ambiguity*) (1947) and in her novel *The Blood of Others* (1945). She later came to criticise the essay, in particular for its inattention to any social context, but she was always to retain a moral stance that the end rarely, if ever, justifies the means. The debate was a crucial theme in *The Mandarins* (1954), where the characters considered the implications of publicising information about Soviet labour camps. In the final analysis, she sided with communism against capitalism, and her critical account of the States in *America Day by Day* (1948) in contrast to her favourable view of the Chinese Revolution in *The Long March* (1957) is witness to her political position, although she and Sartre broke with the Soviet Union 'for good and all' when apprised of the ill treatment of intellectual 'dissidents' and after events in Czechoslovakia in 1968 (*ASD*, p. 352). She continued to believe that only revolution, not bourgeois democracy, could bring the necessary changes in the west. This does not mean, as Whitmarsh suggests (1981, p. 55), that she boycotted the ballot box on principle, as did Sartre. As a woman in France, she only gained the right to vote after the Second World War. Then she voted Communist on occasions, and in the 1980s she voted for the socialist Mitterrand (Schwarzer, 1984, pp. 101&119). By 1982, however, her thoughts on revolution were very cautious. Of the Mitterrand government she had hopes

for a little more justice . . . Quite honestly, I wasn't expecting miracles . . . least of all in this economic climate . . . This socialist government must tread with a very measured and cautious step. It has no option, otherwise it would be staring a revolution in the face. And there can be no question of that at the moment. Personally, I am against a violent, a bloody revolution, at the present time at least. The price would be too high. (Schwarzer, 1984, p. 119)

It was during the Algerian Liberation struggle in the 1950s and early 1960s that de Beauvoir was able to use to effect her position as celebrity intellectual and as a woman by publicising the torture of a young Algerian woman agent and the subsequent attempts to prevent the prosecution of members of the French militia. The published case of *Djamila Boupacha* (1962), deflowered with a bottle by her inquisitors, was documented by her lawyer Gisèle Halimi and introduced by de Beauvoir who, like others involved in the process, took risks in doing so. De Beauvoir argued that this was no exceptional case; it was part of a widespread practice sanctioned at the highest level but concealed by a 'lying propaganda machine' (1963, p. 8). She appealed to the reader

to refuse to countenance a war that dares not speak its true name . . . You can no longer mumble the old excuse 'We didn't know'; and now that you *do* know, can you continue to feign ignorance, or content yourselves with a mere token utterance of horrified sympathy? (1963, p. 19)

On the day of publication, this seemingly armchair act brought death threats. These were not idle ones, since Sartre's home had been bombed twice by those who objected to his and de Beauvoir's support for the Algerian struggle for independence.

The events of May 1968 were to affect de Beauvoir, though to a lesser extent than Sartre:

I am not one of those intellectuals who were deeply shaken by May 1968. In 1962 . . . I was already aware of the contradiction between the intellectual's universal aims and the particularism in which he is imprisoned . . . It worried me once again when I began this book. I make use of language, a universal instrument; I am therefore addressing myself to all men. But I reach only a limited audience. (*ASD*, p. 229)

De Beauvoir was sympathetic to the students who occupied the Sorbonne and who helped to formulate something different from the classical intellectual, who, Sartre disparagingly said, was reduced to signing petitions (Astruc and Contat, 1978, p. 100). Sartre described the new post-1968 intellectuals who would 'have to look for a new way of being with the masses, by turning their backs on whatever specific power they may have' (*ibid.*, p. 102). They were to immerse themselves in the people, something which he complained the communists never allowed.

By the 1970s, de Beauvoir was responding with enthusiasm to some of the tactics of the French Maoist groups who stood for a 'root and branch denial' of the system. They tried to 'focus "fresh forces" in the proletariat – the young, the women, the foreigners . . . They set the problem, the immediate and effectual problem, of the existence of a revolutionary vanguard' (*ASD*, p. 478). This did not mean that de Beauvoir could 'grant China that blind confidence that once the USSR aroused in so many hearts' (*ibid.*, p. 447). She had found the little red book to be a 'quantity of depressingly platitudinous elementary truths' (*ibid.*, p. 445).

A number of Maoist newspapers, run on collective lines, faced legal problems and the threat of imprisonment for those involved, so de Beauvoir and Sartre offered themselves as nominal editors of *L'Idiot International*, in her case, and *La Cause du Peuple* in his. Copies of the latter were distributed by them in the streets of Paris to cause confusion among the authorities who were reluctant to arrest and imprison them. De Beauvoir subsequently distanced herself from *L'Idiot International* and from the individual Maoist, turned religious, whom she considered was exerting an unreal influence on Sartre (*Adieux*, pp. 119–20).

More significant, a new direct form of political participation opened for de Beauvoir with the Women's Liberation Movement. In this it was possible to find some common solidarity as a woman, despite differences of class, race and culture. These activities for the first time, by definition, excluded Sartre. She could participate and be seen to do so in her own right. The boundaries of the political were redefined. Anne Whitmarsh inadvertently reveals the orthodox male definition of the political when describing how, from 1970, de Beauvoir

had become involved in quite a different range of activities which were *not strictly political* . . . These included all kinds of campaigning for better social conditions . . . from prison reform to the treatment of old people, the most important thing being the emancipation of women. (1981, pp. 129–30; my emphasis)

There was ambivalence towards de Beauvoir in the early movement; some women had asked her to join them, while others accused her of being 'Sartre-fixated' and criticised her for writing in a male publication like *Les Temps Modernes* (Schwarzer, 1984, p. 13).

The first women's groups in France were founded in 1970. The MLF (Mouvement de la Libération des Femmes) arranged for three hundred and forty-three women, including de Beauvoir, to declare that they had had an (illegal) abortion. De Beauvoir marched with the several thousand women in 1971 demanding the right to legal abortion. French women were experimenting with the new suction method and de Beauvoir offered her flat for this purpose, again using celebrity status as provocation to the authorities. She proposed a League of Women's Rights, assisted in some of the new publications and began thinking about women's subordination in new areas; for example, sexism in everyday language.

Some of her former political tactics were carried over; for example, the use of her celebrity status. But instead of being faced by the bureaucratic meetings that had so bored her in the past, she embraced these new gatherings of women as more innovative. She met regularly with groups of seven or eight women in intimate domestic settings. Nothing, in Schwarzer's opinion, was too radical for her (*ibid.*, p. 15). She was prepared to redefine her position in relation to feminism. Whereas she had distanced herself from the label feminist in the past – she had considered it to be reformist – she now considered that women needed an autonomous movement rather than simply waiting upon socialism. The new women's liberation movement was looking for more than equal access to male privilege. This new concern for a separate autonomous movement did not, of course, mean neglecting the class struggle: 'They should both be carried on together' (*ASD*, p. 491). The proceeds of de Beauvoir's celebrated interview in 1972 in which she declared herself 'a feminist' went towards hiring rooms for a mass meeting to denounce the crimes against women (Schwarzer, 1984).

At the time I was surprised by de Beauvoir's interview. I had never understood *The Second Sex* and its author to be non-feminist; the interpretation of the word feminism by myself and many others, I suspect, had no rigid institutional boundaries. In the interview, de Beauvoir had chosen to limit the label feminist to organised groups which were 'reformist and legalistic' (Schwarzer, 1984, p. 29). Similarly Juliet Mitchell corralled the feminists of the past, and then presented a rigid dichotomy between 'radical' feminists and socialists, in which the former apparently considered that socialism had nothing to offer women (1971). De Beauvoir later reproduced Mitchell's dichotomy (*ASD*, p. 492). This interpretation of the concept of feminism may well have reflected the new, radical, anti-Marxist feminism of North America in the early seventies. But to suggest that feminism had been seen as incompatible with socialism in the past was to write off with a stroke of the pen the commitment and struggle of thousands of socialist women who also defined themselves as feminist. Perhaps the restricted definition of feminism to one that was anti-socialist or concerned with reformist action associated with male-dominated institutions provided a rationale for the new feminists' former 'bad faith' and past complacency towards gender.

The testimony of socialist suffragettes like Sylvia Pankhurst and those survivors we were fortunate to meet in the fifties and sixties bore witness to the continuous links between feminism and socialism. The suffragettes' innovative and violent tactics which brought them injury, imprisonment and death were neither 'reformist' nor 'legalistic'. Many women had also imagined revolution and changes beyond the ballot box. Later, in the fifties and early sixties, self-defined feminists were submerged within socialist groups and disarmament campaigns. For a variety of reasons they had little choice. Some worked at institutional changes as part of a combined strategy. And whether or not de Beauvoir approved, we used her words.

The first distorted and inaccurate impressions of the 1970s women's movement which reached me were of a rebellion by women who had suddenly realised that marriage wasn't the fulfilment they had hoped. Since, thanks to de Beauvoir, I had chosen to reject marriage and maternity, I could remain loftily detached. The conditions for this detachment were intensified by my immersion in anthropological fieldwork among an oppressed minority – Gypsies, who were far from the metropolitan conference circuit.

The choice of social anthropology was in part a resolution to the class, race and gender constraints of my past. A number of women have felt at home in social anthropology because their marginality within their own culture has encouraged a creative scepticism and a desire to look elsewhere. This form of emancipation proved more instructive than the lessons of the loners and outsiders of the fifties. My friend Margaret was also by this time far from her own culture, in Africa and making a film with Frelimo, the movement for the liberation of Mozambique. Whereas some western women sought another perspective on their own oppression in the crowded company of strangers who were to become friends and associates, de Beauvoir had earlier sought escape from her own culture in a depopulated nature and then in extensive travel.

It was thanks to the intellectual labour and solidarity of other women anthropologists whom I encountered on my return to the culture of academia that the 1970s women's movement made sense: a new feminism shaped my understanding of Gypsy women, fieldwork and academic and political practice (Okely, 1975a). And I continued to draw on de Beauvoir (Okely, 1975b).

For thousands of women likewise, *The Second Sex* made new or changed sense in the late sixties and the seventies. It was passed back to de Beauvoir who in turn engaged with the new literature (*ASD*, pp. 191–5). She warned against the new cult of motherhood, the glorification of 'natural' feminine qualities and the equation of ecology with women. In this respect she dissociated herself from those radical feminists who believe in an 'essential' female nature. While other feminists would also agree with her, they nonetheless point to many qualities among women which arise from their common conditions: for example, the association of women with nurturing and mutual support. Here de Beauvoir continued to be ambivalent. The positive aspects of women's experience were not reassessed. Just as male qualities had been idealised in *The Second Sex* and the heroes in her novels not scrutinised for patriarchal values (see Evans, 1985, ch. 4), so she continued to hold back from a new, radical critique of the masculine domain:

> We mustn't refuse to take on the qualities that are termed masculine! We must be ready to take the risk of involving ourselves in this male world . . . Of course, this way a woman runs the risk of betraying other women, and of betraying feminism . . . But the other way, she runs the risk of suffocating in 'femininity'. (Schwarzer, 1984, p. 116)

She continued to be sceptical of mere piecemeal reforms and the introduction of 'token' women into a few positions of power. Twelve years after the rise of the women's movement, she was a realist about the extent to which feminism had reached the majority of women, beyond the specific campaigns like the demand for abortion. Feminism now faced a backlash because of unemployment and because it threatened male privilege (*ibid.*, p. 115).

There is here a change of tone from the sense of isolation described in *The Force of Circumstance* (quoted above). The absence of women friends, after the death of Zaza in her youth, and in the ensuing years when men were her significant companions, seemed no longer to be a feature of her life by the 1980s. De Beauvoir found new friendships with women, especially that with a young philosophy lecturer, Sylvie le Bon. But as had always been the case, she had few close women friends of her own generation.

Although de Beauvoir found a changed companionship with women, she did not appear to have re-evaluated the extent to which she had lived as intellectual, divorced from experience or practice beyond her class and culture. This practical isolation had affected both the theory and content of her work. Neither

Whitmarsh nor Evans in their assessment of her politics (see above) questions whether there were implications for the ethnographic content of her writing. The one finds de Beauvoir lacking in terms of orthodox and public political action, dismissing many of her informal activities as 'not strictly political' (1981, p. 129). By contrast, Evans concentrates her political critique on de Beauvoir's final programme. We should also be reminded, I suggest, that theory and content reflect the writer's lived experience and daily political practice.

Despite the author's intentions, *The Second Sex* focused on the experience of the bourgeoisie and its fringes. The first-hand references to the United States show a similar concern. That de Beauvoir should tend to exclude a perspective from the experience of those beyond her acquaintance is consistent with her existentialist emphasis on knowledge arising from each individual's specific circumstances. Her error was to universalise from that single position. This is still not unusual. In recent years, deference has been given to grand theories of feminism which in their proud abstractions mask the culturally specific experience of their authors. At the same time, these abstractions lack the specific detail which de Beauvoir displayed in such abundance.

De Beauvoir's isolation from the mass of women outside her class has some similarities with a Leninist notion of the vanguard elite. In *The Mandarins*, de Beauvoir reveals the extraordinary separation of the left wing and politically committed intelligentsia from the proletariat. The very title confirms their position. The political and moral dilemmas of whether the intellectual journalists should publish details of the Soviet labour camps were explored in a vacuum. The mandarins recognised the power vested in the possession of privileged knowledge which they could choose to withhold. The debate was not conducted with individuals at the grassroots; there is hardly a glimpse of the working-class readership of the group's paper, just the following: 'He sighed. It made him happy to see workers buying *L'Espoir* at the corner stand every morning' (1960, p. 473). For the character Henri, a major dilemma is whether he should devote himself to writing in terms of aesthetic ideals or immerse himself in books on political economy. The choice was one between different intellectual pursuits. Like that of de Beauvoir, Henri's view of political action was associated with formal structures. It did not include social relations beyond the élite:

The Resistance was one thing, politics another. And Henri had no great passion for politics. He knew what a movement Dubreuilh had in mind would mean: committees, conferences, congresses, meetings, talk, and still more talk. And it meant endless manoeuvring, . . . lost time, infuriating concessions, sombre boredom. Nothing could be more repulsive to him. Running a newspaper, that was the kind of work he enjoyed. (1960, pp. 17–18)

There are several possible ways of breaking the tendency to interpret the world from a single cultural and class perspective and overcoming the limitations of the individual's personal and historical position. One might be through yet more reading; another is through a change in direct experience and practice, however modest and elusive its results. For all Simone Weil's anarchic individualism, as sister student at the élite Ecole Normale, she showed a way in France of reaching beyond the metropolitan intelligentsia and the bourgeoisie. At times, de Beauvoir recognised the gravity of her own isolation from the proletariat (*F Ci*, p. 669 quoted above). Yet since she acknowledged that her readership did not extend beyond a specific range, her celebrity status would not have been a hindrance elsewhere. Even before she had published, she had preferred freedom in 'nature' rather than in social contexts of a different order. Fame brought the facilities for world-wide travel beyond her own culture. Her experience was that of a privileged celebrity. In the States, for her, the way of breaking out of the tourist trap was to have a love affair with a man; the rest was all buildings, as Anne in *The Mandarins* believes:

I'd rather miss a person than stones. . . . I no longer want to wander about in New York as a tourist; I had to live, really live in that city. That way, it would become a little mine and, in turn, I would leave something of myself in it. I had to walk in the streets holding the arm of a man who provisionally at least, would be mine. (1960, p. 410)

Other relationships were succinctly defined: 'I quickly realised that friendships without tomorrows, and the little anguishes of parting, were part of the pleasure of travelling' (1960, p. 408).

Sartre made a regular practice of the shortcut to understanding another culture through a romantic relationship. It is as if women were a more satisfactory gourmet's guide: 'travelling, and women as I travel, have been very important to me . . . when a woman represents a whole country, that makes a great many things to like' (*Adieux*, p. 303). However profound, 'holiday romances' may not change an individual's political and personal practice.

The vacuum between the intelligentsia and the urban proletariat or rural peasantry was one of the key questions raised by the events of '68. The women's liberation movement, while simultaneously pointing to shared gender across class and culture, also made some attempts to support in an active way the struggles of specific groups of women. For example, the movement intervened in the strike by the women night cleaners in Britain and in the setting up of houses for battered women; something with which de Beauvoir was involved.

When de Beauvoir on occasions confronted at first hand other existences among the urban proletariat and peasantry in France, these experiences left a vivid impression. She usually refrained from pursuing them in any deeper way. In 1971 she acknowledged the different perspective which such contact might bring, as in the case when she helped to expose the effects of an industrial accident in the provinces:

this journey taught me a great deal. I met young working women, went into their homes, saw how they lived, listened to them and their families. It was only a very limited experience, because the Méru factories are small undertakings in a rural area and the girls are almost all peasants' daughters; but it gave me a more immediate, realistic view of their way of life than I could ever have obtained from books. (*ASD*, p. 478)

It would be wrong to suggest that de Beauvoir could ever enter fully into the experience of others, but a 'more immediate' participation beyond the metropolitan élites, of whatever country, might have tempered the universalisms in *The Second Sex*. Her novels do not of course show the same tendencies; they remain unashamedly rooted in the metropolitan élites.

Inevitably twenty-five years after a first reading, I make different demands of the mother/mentor de Beauvoir. A reconstructed feminism has changed expectations of any so-called vanguard. The very notion of leaders within a hierarchy has been profoundly questioned by the women's movement which instead builds on a practice of co-operative solidarity and even 'feminine' self-effacement. Yet in the past, de Beauvoir's powerful influence on her female readers is partly explained by her exceptional position in a male-dominated intellectual élite. She found the means and voice to make a critique of the system from which she came. In writing *The Second Sex*, she said she learned that her privileges 'were the result of my having abdicated, in some crucial respects at least, my womanhood'.[1] Whereas she wanted to speak about the conditions of all women, she could only attempt this from a position which entailed solitude among men and an exile from womankind.

Note

1   Gerassi, 1976.

THE WORKS OF SIMONE DE BEAUVOIR

The reader should refer to Claude Francis and Fernande Gontier, *Les écrits de Simone de Beauvoir*, 1979, Paris: Gallimard, for a comprehensive bibliography and collection of assorted articles and hitherto unpublished texts.

The French title is given first, with details of the first edition; it is followed by the date of the first English translation (if one exists) and details of the edition referred to (if different) in this text. All English versions, except for *She Came to Stay*, *The Blood of Others* and the de Sade essay, have male translators.

L'Invitée, 1943, Paris: Gallimard. *She Came to Stay* (1949), 1975, London: Fontana

Pyrrhus et Cinéas, 1944, Paris: Gallimard

Le sang des autres, 1945, Paris: Gallimard. *The Blood of Others*, 1948, London: Secker & Warburg

Les bouches inutiles, 1945, Paris: Gallimard. Play in two acts. First performed 31 October 1945, Théâtre des Carrefours, Paris

Tous les hommes sont mortels, 1946, Paris: Gallimard. *All Men Are Mortal*, 1955, Cleveland: World Publishing Company

Pour une morale de l'ambiguité, 1947, Paris: Gallimard. *The Ethics of Ambiguity*, 1948, New York: Philosophical Library

L'Amérique au jour le jour, 1948, Paris: Morihien. *America Day by Day*, 1957, London: Duckworth

L'existentialisme et la sagesse des nations, 1948, Paris: Nagel

Le deuxième sexe, 2 vols. I *Les faits et les mythes*. II *L'expérience vécue*, 1949, Paris: Gallimard. *The Second Sex* (1953). Transl. Parshley, H. M., 1972, Harmondsworth: Penguin

164   *Simone de Beauvoir*

'MustWeBurnSade?'('Faut-ilbrûlerSade?'),1953,London:PeterNevill

Les mandarins, 1954, Paris: Gallimard. 52nd Prix Goncourt. *The Mandarins* (1957) 1960, London: Fontana/Collins

Privilèges, 1955, Paris: Gallimard

La longue marche, 1957, Paris: Gallimard. *The Long March*, 1958, London: André Deutsch/Weidenfeld & Nicolson

Mémoires d'une jeune fille rangée, 1958, Paris: Gallimard. *Memoirs of a Dutiful Daughter* (1959), 1963, Harmondsworth: Penguin

La force de l'âge, 1960, Paris: Gallimard. *The Prime of Life* (1962), 1965, Harmondsworth: Penguin

Brigitte Bardot and the Lolita Syndrome, 1960, London: André Deutsch/Weidenfeld & Nicolson

Preface to Gisèle Halimi, 1962, *Djamila Boupacha*, Paris: Gallimard. Transl. (1962) 1963, London: Four Square Books

La force des choses, 1963, Paris: Gallimard. *Force of Circumstance* (1965), 1968, Harmondsworth: Penguin

Une mort très douce, 1964, Paris: Gallimard. *A Very Easy Death* (1966), 1969, Harmondsworth: Penguin

Que peut la littérature?, 1965. A symposium, ed. by Buin, Y., Paris: Union Générale d'Editeurs: Collection L'Inédit. Contributions by Simone de Beauvoir, *et al*

Les belles images, 1966, Paris: Gallimard. *Les belles images*, 1969, London: Fontana/Collins

La femme rompue, followed by *Monologue* and *L'âge de discretion*, 1968, Paris: Gallimard. *The Woman Destroyed*, followed by *The Monologue* and *The Age of Discretion* (1969), 1971, London: Fontana/Collins

La vieillesse, 1970, Paris: Gallimard. *Old Age*, 1972, London: André Deutsch/Weidenfeld & Nicolson

Tout compte fait, 1972, Paris: Gallimard. *All Said and Done* (1974), 1977, Harmondsworth: Penguin

'Queries to Jean-Paul Sartre' (1975), 1976, *New Left Review* (May-June), 97: 71–80

Quand prime le spirituel (written 1935–6), 1979, Paris: Gallimard. *When Things of the Spirit Come First*, 1982, London: André Deutsch/Weidenfeld & Nicolson

Preface to *Le sexisme ordinaire* (1973), 1979 (Introducing the first appearance of the feminist section in *Les temps modernes* from which the articles in the book were taken), Paris: Editions du Seuil

La cérémonie des adieux suivi des *Entretiens avec Jean-Paul Sartre* 1981, Paris: Gallimard. *Adieux – Farewell to Sartre*, 1984, London: Deutsch

Lettres au Castor et à quelques autres, by Sartre, J. P., ed. de Beauvoir, 1983 (Tome I: 1926–1939. Tome II: 1940–1963). Paris: Gallimard

REFERENCES

Works devoted wholly or in part to Simone de Beauvoir

For a comprehensive bibliography of works on Simone de Beauvoir up to 1970, see Cayron, C., 1973. *La nature chez Simone de Beauvoir*, Paris: Gallimard
For a comprehensive bibliography after 1970, excluding most theses and book reviews, see Whitmarsh, A., 1981, *Simone de Beauvoir and the Limits of Commitment*, Cambridge: Cambridge University Press

Abel, E., (ed.), *Writing and Sexual Difference*, Brighton, Harvester Press, 1982
Ardener, E., 'Belief and the Problem of Women' in *Perceiving Women*, (ed.) Ardener, S., London, Dent, (1972) 1975
Ardener, S., 'Sexual Insult and Female Militancy' in *Perceiving Women*, (ed.) Ardener, S., London, Dent, 1975
Ascher, C., *Simone de Beauvoir: A Life of Freedom*, Brighton, Harvester Press, 1981
Astruc, A. and Contat, M., *Sartre by Himself* (text of film), New York, Urizen Books, 1978
Barrett, M., *Women's Oppression Today*, London, Verso, 1980
Barrett, M., 'Rethinking Women's Oppression: A Reply to Brenner and Ramas', *New Left Review*, 146, 1984
Bieber, K., *Simone de Beauvoir*, Boston, Twayne Publishers, 1979
Bloch, J., and Bloch, M., 'Women and the Dialectics of Nature in Eighteenth-century Thought' in McCormack, C., and Strathern, M., (below), 1980
Bourdieu, P., *Outline of a Theory of Practice*, Cambridge, Cambridge University Press, 1977

Brenner, J. and Ramas, M., 'Rethinking Women's Oppression', *New Left Review*, 144, 1984

Breton, A., *Nadja*, Paris, Gallimard, (1926) 1947

Breton, A., *L'Amour Fou*, Paris, Gallimard, 1937

Brown, B., and Adams, P., 'The Feminine Body and Feminist Politics', *M/F*, Number 3, 1979

Brownstein, R., *Becoming a Heroine*, Harmondsworth, Penguin, 1984

Carby, H., 'White Woman Listen! Black Feminism and the boundaries of sisterhood', in *The Empire Strikes Back*, Centre for Contemporary Cultural Studies, University of Birmingham, London, Hutchinson, 1982

▷ Carter, A., 'The Intellectual's Darby and Joan', *New Society*, 28 January 1982: 156–7

Chodorow, N., *The Reproduction of Mothering*, Berkeley, University of California, 1978

Craig, C., 'Simone de Beauvoir's *The Second Sex* in the light of the Hegelian Master-Slave Dialectic and Sartrian Existentialism', PhD, University of Edinburgh, 1979

Dayan, J. and Ribowska, M., *Simone de Beauvoir* (text of film), Paris, Gallimard, 1978

Delmar, R., 'Looking Again at Engels's *Origin of the Family, Private Property and the State*' in *The Rights and Wrongs of Women*, (eds) Mitchell, J., and Oakley, A., Harmondsworth, Penguin, 1976

Dworkin, A., *Pornography: Men Possessing Women*, London, The Women's Press, 1981

Ellmann, M., *Thinking about Women*, London, Virago, (1968) 1979

Evans, M., 'Views of Women and Men in the Work of Simone de Beauvoir', *Women's Studies International Quarterly*, 3: 395–404, 1980

Evans, M., *Simone de Beauvoir. A Feminist Mandarin*, Tavistock, London, 1985

Firestone, S., *The Dialectic of Sex*, London, Paladin, (1970) 1972

Francis, C., and Gontier, S., *Simone de Beauvoir*, Paris, Perrin, 1985

Friedan, B., *The Feminine Mystique*, Harmondsworth, Penguin (1963) 1965

Gardiner, J., 'On Female Identity and Writing by Women' in Abel, E., (above), 1982

Gerassi, J., 'Simone de Beauvoir. *The Second Sex* 25 years later', *Society*, 79–80, 1976 (Jan-Feb)

Gilbert, S., and Gubar, S., (eds), *The Madwoman in the Attic*, Newhaven and London, Yale University Press, 1979

▽ Hardwick, E., 'The Subjection of Women', *Partisan Review* 20 (3), May-June: 321–31, 1953

Harris, O., 'Complementarity and Conflict: An Andean view of women and men' in *Sex and age as principles of social differentiation*, (ed.) La Fontaine, J., London, Academic Press, 1978

Harris, O., 'The Power of Signs: gender, culture and the wild in the Bolivian Andes', in McCormack, C., and Strathern, M., (below), 1980

Heilbrun, C., *Reinventing Womanhood*, London, Gollancz, 1979

Irigaray, L., 'Women's Exile', interview with Luce Irigaray, *M/F*, No. 1: 62–76, 1977

Jacobus, M., (ed.), *Women Writing and Writing about Women*, London, Croom Helm, 1979

Jacobus, M., 'The Question of Language: Men of Maxims and The Mill on the Floss', in Abel, E., (above), 1982

Jardine, A., 'Interview with Simone de Beauvoir', *Signs* 5(2): 224–36, 1979

Jelinek, E., (ed.), *Women's Autobiography*, Bloomington and London, Indiana University Press, 1980

Keefe, T., *Simone de Beauvoir: a study of her writings*, London, Harrap, 1984

Kristeva, J., *About Chinesewomen*, London, Marion Boyars, 1977

La Fontaine, J., 'Ritualisation of Women's Life-Crises in Bugisu' in La Fontaine, J., (ed.), *The Interpretation of Ritual*, London, Tavistock, 1972

Lessing, D., *The Golden Notebook*, London, Granada, (1962) 1971 (New Preface)

McCormack, C. and Strathern, M., *Nature, Culture and Gender*, Cambridge, Cambridge University Press, 1980

Millett, K., *Sexual Politics*, London, Virago, (1970) 1977

Mitchell, J., *Woman's Estate*, Harmondsworth, Penguin, 1971

Mitchell, J., *Psychoanalysis and Feminism*, Harmondsworth, Allen Lane, 1974

Mitchell, J., *Women: The Longest Revolution*, London, Virago, 1984

Moers, E., *Literary Women*, London, The Women's Press, (1977) 1978

Moi, T., 'Jealousy and Sexual Difference', *Feminist Review* 11: 53–68, 1982

Oakley, A., *Taking it Like a Woman*, London, Cape, 1984

Okely, J., 'The Spectre of Feminism', *The Messenger* (4): 4–5, 1963

Okely, J., 'The Self and Scientism', *Journal of Anthropology Society of Oxford (JASO)*, Trinity term, 1975a

Okely, J., 'Gypsy Women: Models in Conflict' in *Perceiving Women* (ed.) Ardener, S., London, Dent, 1975b

Okely, J., 'Privileged, Schooled and Finished: Boarding Education for

168   *Simone de Beauvoir*

Girls' in *Defining Females*, (ed.) Ardener, S., London, Croom Helm, 1978

Okely, J., *The Traveller-Gypsies*, Cambridge, Cambridge University Press, 1983

Okely, J., 'Sexuality and Biology in *The Second Sex*', paper given to the Social Anthropology Inter-Collegiate Seminar, London University, 1984

Ortner, S., 'Is Female to Male as Nature is to Culture?' in *Woman, Culture and Society*, (eds) Rosaldo, M. and Lamphere, L. Stanford, Stanford University Press, 1974

Pocock, D., 'The Idea of a Personal Anthropology', paper presented to the Decennial Conference of the Association of Social Anthropologists, Oxford, 1973

Rich, A., 'Compulsory Heterosexuality and Lesbian Existence', *Signs* 5, 1980

Rich, A., *Of Woman Born*, London, Virago, (1977) 1979

Rowbotham, S., *Woman's Consciousness, Man's World*, Harmondsworth, Penguin 1973

Sacks, K., 'Engels Revisited: Women, the organisation of production, and private property' in *Woman, Culture and Society*, (eds) Rosaldo, M., and Lamphere, L., Stanford, Stanford University Press, 1974

Sartre, J. P., *La nausée (Nausea)*, Paris, Gallimard, 1938

Sartre, J. P., *L'Etre et le néant (Being and Nothingness)*, Paris, Gallimard, 1943

Sartre, J. P., *Les Mots (Words)*, Paris, Gallimard, 1964

Sartre, J. P., *Lettres au Castor et à quelques autres*, (ed.) de Beauvoir, Paris, Gallimard, 1983

Sartre, J. P., *War Diaries*, London, Verso, (1983) 1984

Sayers, J., *Biological Politics*, London, Tavistock, 1982

Schwarzer, A., *Simone de Beauvoir Today: Conversations 1972–1982*, London, Chatto & Windus/The Hogarth Press, 1984

Sciama, L., 'The Problem of Privacy in Mediterranean Anthropology' in *Women and Space*, (ed.) Ardener, S., London, Croom Helm, 1981

Showalter, E., *A Literature of Their Own*, London, Virago, (1977) 1978

Simons, M., 'The Silencing of Simone de Beauvoir: guess what's missing from *The Second Sex*', *Women's Studies International Forum* 6 (5): 559–64, 1983

Spacks, P. M., *The Female Imagination*, New York, Avon, (1972) 1975

Spark, M., *The Prime of Miss Jean Brodie*, Harmondsworth, Penguin (1961) 1965

Stubbs, P., *Women and Fiction: Feminism and the Novel 1880–1920*, Brighton, Harvester Press, 1979

Walters, M., 'The Rights and Wrongs of Women: Mary Wollstonecraft,

Harriet Martineau and Simone de Beauvoir' in *The Rights and Wrongs of Women*, (eds) Oakley, A., and Mitchell, J., Harmondsworth, Penguin, 1976

Walters, M., *The Nude Male*, Harmondsworth, Penguin, 1979

Whitmarsh, A., *Simone de Beauvoir and the Limits of Commitment*, Cambridge, Cambridge University Press, 1981

Wilson, E., *Only Halfway to Paradise: Women in Post-War Britain 1945–1968*, London, Tavistock, 1980

Woolf, V., *A Room of One's Own*, London, The Hogarth Press, 1929

INDEX